Narrative Design

INTERKULTURELLER DIALOG

Herausgegeben von Annemarie Profanter

BAND 6

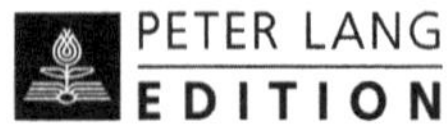

Giulia Cordin

Narrative Design

The Designer as an Instigator of Changes

With an Introduction by Formafantasma

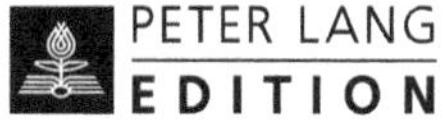

Bibliographic Information published by the Deutsche Nationalbibliothek
The Deutsche Nationalbibliothek lists this publication in the Deutsche Nationalbibliografie; detailed bibliographic data is available in the internet at http://dnb.d-nb.de.

Library of Congress Cataloging-in-Publication Data
Names: Cordin, Giulia, 1989- author.
Title: Narrative design : the designer as an instigator of changes / Giulia Cordin ; With an Introduction by Formafantasma.
Description: New York : Peter Lang, 2016. | Series: Interkultureller Dialog ; Band 6 | Includes bibliographical references
Identifiers: LCCN 2016005891 | ISBN 9783631660928
Subjects: LCSH: Design services. | Design—Social aspects.
Classification: LCC NK1173 .C67 2016 | DDC 745.4—dc23 LC record available at http://lccn.loc.gov/2016005891

Translation: Ryan Anthony Licata

Photos: © Giulia Cordin

The publication was financially supported by Michael Seeber, President of the Leitner AG

ISSN 1866-752X
ISBN 978-3-631-66092-8 (Print)
E-ISBN 978-3-653-05875-8 (E-Book)
DOI 10.3726/978-3-653-05875-8

Peter Lang Edition is an Imprint of Peter Lang GmbH.

Peter Lang – Frankfurt am Main · Bern · Bruxelles · New York · Oxford · Warszawa · Wien

This publication has been peer reviewed.

www.peterlang.com

Index

Preface

The content of the book *Narrative Design. The designer as an instigator of changes* is derived from a study developed for the bachelor degree in Design and Arts presented in July 2013 at the Free University of Bolzano. The project aims to analyze the theme of the stereotype as a process with a strong social and cultural importance in our contemporary society through a design approach. The stereotype has been acquired as an abstract design incentive through which one can understand how reported knowledge on other countries are formed and how these images influence a future encounter with the Other. Each designed object aims to produce a three-dimensional visualization of the stereotype through a free interpretation of the phenomenon itself.

In November 2014, following the appointed graduation prize within the Forum "Kulturen im Dialog"[1] regarding the relationship between peoples, I had the opportunity to carry out my research and to publish the results of my work. The book integrates the project by opening a discussion on themes and emerging strategies about the role of the designer today and presents historical and contemporary perspectives through design practices that are committed to provide proposals and solutions to social issues. By the analysis of several case studies, the research displays a method and an approach to design as narrative instrument, a design practice capable of conveying messages and content beyond the functionality and the aesthetic of the objects. Products and processes that fill our

1 The Fourth Forum for Young Graduates "Kulturen im Dialog" was organized by Prof. DDr. Mag. MSc Annemarie Profanter at the Free University of Bolzano on November 28th 2014. The project addressed to undergraduates, graduates and postgraduates, ranged across all disciplines and universities; the research presented, theoretical or empirical, had to deal with issues regarding development policy, interculture, migration, integration, international development, business ethics, development cooperation, peace education and conflict mediation. Five of the submitted thesis were selected and presented to the public in front of a committee composed by Prof. Walter Lorenz (Rector of the Free University of Bolzano), Prof. Gerhard Glüher (Dean of the Faculty of Design and Art of Bolzano), Prof. Walter Schicho (Institute of International Development, University of Vienna), Prof. Anna-Aluffi Pentini (Faculty of Education Unibz and Roma Tre University), Prof. Stefan Franz Schubert, (Faculty of Economics, Unibz), Dr. Martina Rienzner (Institute of International Development, University of Vienna), Prof. Annemarie Profanter (Faculty of Education, Unibz).

daily life experiences and which assume a value of cultural medium to explore and propose complex issues through the artistic dimension. Objects charged with a strong narrative vocation capable of telling a complex story even before reacting to a practical function.

Doom

Introduction by Formafantasma

With industrialization hand-made production had to confront the capabilities of the machine: faster, cheaper and comparatively perfect. The machine in itself represents what humans will never be able to produce: not only a perfect original, but also its reproduction. Furthermore, with the Modern movement the technical capacity of mechanical reproduction became a tool for what was intended to be a democratic revolution. Modernism began with the urge to give new meaning to industrial products and it evolved into a social and cultural transformation and ended with the idea of "international style." Geometric forms, typical elements of the international style, are symbols of the idealistic and universal pretension central to the movement. In this context, craft seemed to belong to the past: expensive, decorative and representative of a local culture. It is important to note that the aversion of the Modern movement to decoration has been misunderstood and perceived as a universal dictat. Instead, the rejection of decoration was based on the idea that machine made products needed their own approach and language. Inevitably new taste influenced craft that reacted in two different ways: imitating past or imitating industry and its style, removing as much as possible any trace of handcrafted work. Craft then survived the wave of the 'new machines' or cooperating with industry in the best of cases (in Italy there are several great examples of this phenomenon) or becoming tourist attractions. In earlier times, shops as we know them today were rare in the countryside. If a farmer needed an item he went directly to the craftsman to obtain it. The final design depended on the social relationship between craftsman and customer. Based on these specific needs and their evolution craft evolved. When it became possible to buy industrial-produced products around the eighteenth and nineteenth centuries, the craftsman was immediately affected. Nowadays in many instances the tourist is the substitute for the traditional customer (Caltagirone in Sicily and Delft in The Netherlands are two good examples). Generally speaking, tourists are the only consumers who still visit workshops to buy craft items, which are often not used for their functional purposes, but rather to evoke an experience (the trip) or the formalized idea of a place (souvenir: from the Latin word sovvenire: to evoke).

This is, of course, a simplified overview of the complex relationship between industry and craft and we all know how the entire history of design as a discipline has seen designers successfully collaborating with craftsmen from Morris and the arts and crafts movement to Memphis until the most contemporary examples. In this sense the renewed interest for craft isn't exactly a novelty but it definitely defines a change in the needs of society. Never before has so much been produced, yet the physical distance between us and the fruit of our labours has also increased. Goods are produced 'elsewhere' and perceived as much without history and information as people feel to be without identity and locality. In today's climate of consumption, global production systems are growing out of control. As a reaction, people have started to claim locality in the name of sustainability. Within this framework local production is becoming necessary not only for environmental issues but for psychological sustainability: to cut out the distance between humankind and production helps to reconnect people to their culture. Understanding the intrinsic meaning of objects helps us to know ourselves better and to externalize ourselves. In this sense the contemporary fetish for craft is assuming almost a symbolic value where hand-made goods represent a more sustainable and human way of producing. We feel this is a trend that is already evolving, leaving behind nostalgia and romanticism and the idea of supremacy of the man-made over the machine-made, while maintaining its core: the necessity for a more transparent, local and relevant production where the superfluous and the un-ethical is despicable.

Often we are asked if we are interested in industrial production and in which way our work responds to the idea of democratic design (the concept has been recently revived and affected by a great dose of nostalgia) since the majority of our objects are produced in a limited amount. The answer is in the 99 percent of all instances based on an idea of democratic design that could be afforded only by a very limited amount of people living in the so called western world, which is producing the majority of worldwide Co2 emissions. In this moment we are developing products that will be industrially produced and are designed based on a series of principles that include durability, reduction of volume for shipping, functionality and a design as timeless as possible to encourage a long lasting bond between user and object. Even if designed according to the aforementioned grid, these objects will never be a response to the real needs of the planet and the species inhabiting it.

As designers we are wondering on a daily bases how could we be interested in industrial production in the same way as architects, engineers and designers were in post-war Europe when the need of reconstruction was at its peak.

In this specific moment in time how can we be enthralled by the idea that our work might be bought by millions of people all over the world if what we design is a vase or a chair?

How can we still believe in the existing economic model when it is the major cause of an ever-accelerating descent towards ecological doom?

We consider the work we have developed so far as an investigation of different ideas which are not yet offering solutions but more problematizing economic, social, and political issues.

Our fascination for objects lies in their ability to represent human history and even possible futures.

We see Design as a discipline meant to questions and envision social, cultural, and even political changes.

Narrative Design

The designer as an instigator of changes

Designers are usually considered as problem solvers: their function is to make a process more efficient or to make a product better or more beautiful. But what if instead of solving problems they posed them?

When in the Middle Ages Sicily was affected by drought, the locals asked St. Joseph, their patron, to save them from dying of famine by making rain. The rain came and in his honour a big feast was organized. Decorated and complex loaves were prepared as a thanksgiving by the women and made cook in the different island countries. Since then every year the anniversary is celebrated by the residents of Salemi, a small town in the southwest of Sicily; a tradition which has impressed and inspired the studio Formafantasma represented by the designers Andrea Trimarchi and Simone Farresin.

From the reinterpretation of this story arose the project "Autarchy", a collection of containers, vases and lamps, naturally dried or baked at a low temperature, products with a bio – material developed on the same mixture of Sicilian bread.

"What people ask of design is that it finds solutions, and that it simplifies the existing ones. Instead, our projects do the opposite: they ask questions, and seek to initiate a discussion." (Spike Art Magazine, *Studio Formafantasma avantgarde post-industrial aesthetic,* Web) explained Formafantasma. The objects of the collection "Autarchy" represent poor and simple products, of archetypal forms revisited and made contemporary, which describe a simple world, an anonymous way to produce consumer goods through cultivation, in a hypothetical scenario of serene and self-imposed embargo. But what Faresin and Trimarchi realized with "Autarchy" goes beyond the mere aesthetic or functional value of the product. Their products compel one to question systems and materials of contemporary production, proposing scenarios and solutions that force a difference. In this sense, design could have a strong narrative added value: products produce meanings, which are not only about functionality or production processes, but also emotions and present and historical knowledge.

If in the last century design stood for functionality, efficiency and pleasant to the eye aesthetics, since the end of the twentieth century, designers, or at least some of them, have started to contract out from the laws of industrial production, and, supported by a growing awareness of their tools, have started to personally construct the opportunities and the conditions in which to intervene, design and communicate, called upon to move within contexts that are increasingly less certain and less linear. This, for example, accounts for the growing commitment to lending their voice to contents and stories that lie beyond the market rationale by self-initiated projects; the use of design as a form of research and inquiry; the interest in experimenting and connecting closely related activities, to reach a diversified audience.

"Design is a territory that is difficult to take in with just one glance. Necessarily heteronomous, it presents itself not so much as a self-contained region with accurately defined confines, but rather as a nucleus from which and towards which different paths spread out as they relate to a variety of contexts, drawing a plurality of worlds" (Camuffo, Dalla Mura 2011). "Stimulated by big and small economic, social, and technological changes – ranging from industrial crises to the phenomenon of globalization – over the past decade designers have explored and acquired different motivations and means to ply their trade" (id.). Some designers don't design practical products anymore, but create exploratory prototypes – not of new products but of a new kind of product. "They operate in a cultural context, working both on commissioned and free projects. They are critical, politically engaged and set new rules for their field, such as the assertion of having a non-neutral position; the attention turned towards the process and construction of experiences, rather than on the finished products; the stress placed on collaboration and participation beyond dualism such as question-answer, problem – solution, designer – client; the overcoming of disciplinary boundaries in favour of cross-pollination with other sectors and practises"(id.).

Once designers step away from industrial production and the marketplace we enter the realm of the fictional: through narration, designers come into an arena that was previously reserved for artists; a space where provocations and critical observations, but also manual and handcrafted excellence, become dominant.

It is called critical design. Sometimes conceptual or speculative design. Whatever the name, it is design with a new function: to make you think. It is design that makes us aware of who we are but also who we can be. It means that a problem or an idea is constantly questioned and that all the options are kept open, however radical the solutions may be.

It has a short but rich history and it is a place where many interconnected and not very well understood forms of design happen. It is a history with multiple identities, with a variety of experiences and names that have been shared to a greater or lesser extent, and that have gradually shaped the definition of design as something poised between art and industry, free expression and problem-solving, creativity and the standard.

The separation from the marketplace creates a parallel design channel free from market pressures and available to explore ideas and issues. These could be new possibilities for design itself; new aesthetic possibilities for technology; social, cultural, and ethical implications for scientific and technological research; or large-scale social and political issues such as democracy, sustainability, and alternatives to our current model of market.

"Similar experiences and directions have not just contributed to redesigning the reference map for design, broadening its scope of action, but have also attracted other visitors. Rather than dwelling upon the definition of a technical or professional specialization, an important segment of critical discourse has increasingly focused on the interpretation that can be given to as well as on the use that can be made of tools and methods, that is, on the role that the designer can play through them, as a subject capable of starting up and building relations, and as author, producer, entrepreneur and agent, taking active part in society and contemporary culture." (id.)

Trained to move among different languages and media that pervade our daily lives, designers actually find themselves in the ideal position to read, filter and channel a social and cultural fabric that develops by communicating itself. You can expect a good designer to pick up on the signals that characterize a particular moment, to analyse them, and find a meaningful way of translating them, trusting not only their intuition but also taking scientific and theoretical insights into account.

Designing a chair of which thousands can be produced is no more an interesting starting point. Designers prefer to think about new ways of sitting. Which does not, however, exclude the fact that such product exploration can ultimately lead to a chair of which thousands can be produced.

It is a new sensibility which tries to bring design on a different level. The fact that most of these proposals come from Great Britain and the Netherlands is no coincidence, because they are nowadays at the epicentre of a Crafts Renaissance. The UK was the first place where mechanization established itself, and where, subsequently, its limits and its potential have been challenged. In the second half of the nineteenth century, the industrial revolution momentarily separated the process of "good design" from the process of production. The issue of ethics in the design and in the production was raised by the Arts and Crafts Movement and its protagonists traced an ideal swing between two extremes: on the virtuous side of this movement stood the craftsman, independent producer of ideas; on the other side, placed on an industrial scale, was the producer, a mere actuator and transformer of the materials. This event left a significant mark on the world of design. Over the past twenty years, by binding to the new conditions of the world and the market, handcrafting returned to creep with increasing force into the theoretical debate and practice of design. The interest in crafts goes beyond a nostalgic flirtation with traditions. Crafts stand for thoughtful product design, and are not aimed at a quick commercial turnover but rather focused on the longstanding relationship between product and user. The handicraft production is achieved after a long process of thought and critique and is not an end in itself but a means of achieving a more sustainable design. Old techniques are reconsidered without prejudice and accepted as contemporary options. Art and functionality obviously go hand in hand in this design, but in this case art transcends the purely aesthetic value and excites, disturbs, invites uncomfortable thoughts. The designs are not always immediately functional things, but they may show possible futures. The pace of research and technological innovation has changed enormously over the past quarter of a century and the present moment is very important for design, because it is not only the technology and computer science that is progressing, but also the idea of sustainability, a topic that becomes part of the work of many designers. For this reason many designers are increasingly focusing on behaviour rather than on objects. The work of design today is much closer to imagining possible and plausible futures, rather than generate useful items (Ted X, *Paola Antonelli treats design as art*, Web).

Useful objects have a potential that goes beyond functionality. The story can rise above the objects itself. The function of design lies mainly in its communicative strength in the story that goes beyond basic functionality and that is sometimes even at odds with it. You can no longer formulate the function solely in terms of use or comfort. Sometimes it even lies – paradoxically – in its non-functionality, especially in the extent to which products appeal above all to your imagination.

There are many designers who find the question more interesting than the answer: they consciously avoid designing new forms, but rather add a new dimension, a different function or a different story. Often the research results alone are not interesting, but they start with them to do something. For instance, a different sense of awareness: they share knowledge through an end product. This critical approach to designing has evolved into an open mentality in which nothing is predetermined and everything is up for discussion. It utilises both traditional artisanal methods and digital production techniques, but it is always singular and well thought-out. It is a conceptual and thoughtful approach providing new tools to achieve different solutions. These are objects charged with a strong narrative vocation, capable of telling a complex story even before answering a practical function.

It is a design with some dominant themes, such as the artisanal working method, the flirtation with art, the conceptual research, the innovative prototypes and production techniques. It is a critical design – problem finding, which asks questions and opens debate. It is in the service of society, which shows how the world could be and tries to change us to suit it. It is a humorous design, both provocative and conceptual, which makes us think along some dominant themes, such as the attention to the phenomena of globalization, problems concerning environment and poverty, the depletion of natural resources; and also contemporary and concrete issues, which require an investigation and a clear stance.

These designers are aware that complex issues cannot be solved with a product, but their mission is to create awareness. The commitment, with which they work hard to make even small improvements in living conditions, opens new perspectives not only to the practice of design, but also in politics and in the management of public and private sectors. These designers appeal to the imagination of the viewer: they often take the form of scenarios, often starting with a what-if question, with the intention of opening up spaces of debate and discussion. They are by necessity provocative, intentionally simplified, and fictional. Their fictional nature requires viewers to suspend their disbelief and allow their imaginations to wander, to momentarily forget how things are now, and wonder about how things could be.

Normally these products are very beautiful, well refined, interesting. In order for the concept to be transmitted, it is necessary that people be interested and attracted by the objects. In this sense, there is, therefore, the first level encounter whereby it is possible to appreciate the external shape of the products, the choice of materials, and the recourse to more or less interesting forms. Then, however, there is a whole series of levels which may be further analysed. The situation of consumption is not the most important. It is possible to pass ideas on to people in a more complex and more visionary way, creating a context and a background around the project.

It is very difficult to finance this kind of design activity and there are limited opportunities but it is needed. It feeds the profession's imagination and it opens up new possibilities, not only for technology, materials, and manufacturing, but also for narrative, meaning, and the rethinking of everyday life. Rather than waiting for commissions from industry or seeking out market gaps for new products, designers could work together with curators, entrepreneurs, anthropologists and other professionals, independently of industry, to bring beauty and wisdom not only to the design practice, but also to the political and socio – cultural management of our lives.

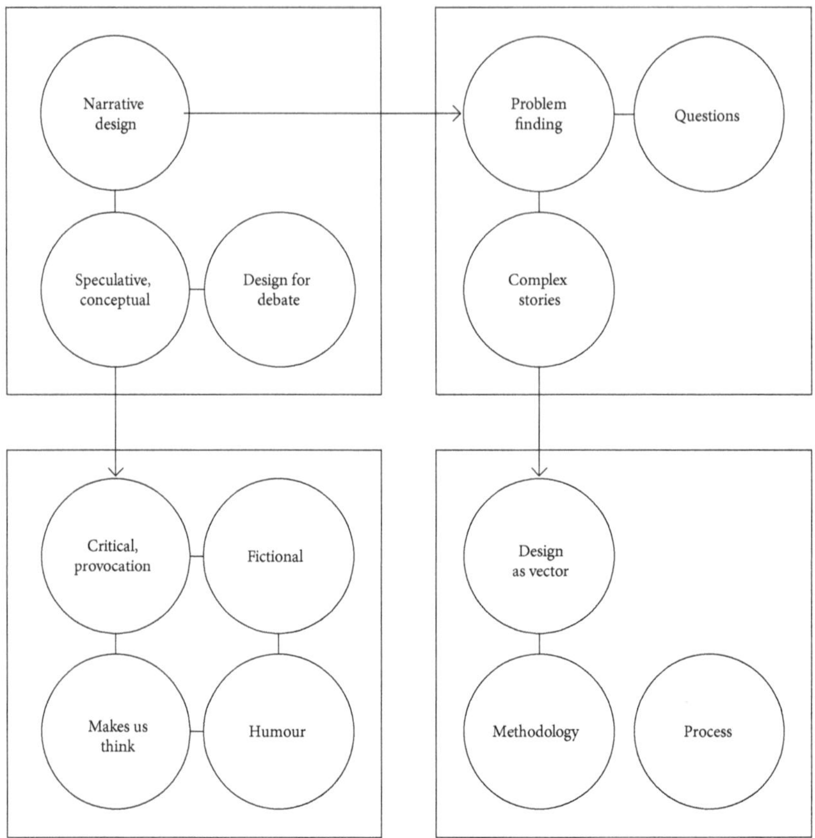

Fig. 1: Narrative Design Features.

Examples of these trends can be found all over the world, but a group of designers from the Netherlands has in recent years responded to these expectations with an unanimity that merits particular attention. A climate favourable to an alternative movement had been created in the Netherlands. There were hardly any commissions from industry, but the government provided grants for experiments and research. The funding enabled the Dutch designers to pursue different interests, free from pressure of industry, which has made the big difference between their experience and that of colleagues abroad. Not all of these designers are formally associated with one another; some belong to different generations or have attended different schools. Although these groups are often only nominal – formed in a spirit of strength in unity, nonetheless, they all share a similar sensitivity.

The same institutions invest in this direction, where forward-thinking policies have been activated. Starting from design schools, art galleries and museums, in such places discussion is open and possible. It is rare in Italy that design is adopted as a research tool to investigate or discuss society. The world outside school does not often seem to provide space for design as a self-employed and reflective activity. However, universities and art schools could become platforms for experimentation, speculation and the re-examination of our everyday life. Such as the Design Academy Eindhoven, the hub of speculative, critical, experimental or socially and politically engaged design that has characterized Dutch design production in the last three decades. Another example is the Royal College of Arts in London. Renowned for their education in design, they provide fertile ground for speculative concepts and adventurous experiments, and places where students acquire a way of thinking and designing, where the issue is perhaps less important than the method and the theoretical awareness developed to lay the foundations of future professions.

Also some private galleries – Kreo in Paris and Libby Sellers in London for instance – have been instrumental in giving promising as well as established designers the opportunity to test new ideas in a secure and supportive environment. Progressive institutes offer a selected group of designers the opportunity to extend the boundaries of the discipline in total freedom. Handmade products are still perceived as having more importance, both culturally and economically, and the advantage in displaying such projects in the context of the galleries is the freedom to develop complex and projects, which are often not suitable for mass production.

Even museums have opened up more and more to design. "Today it no longer makes sense to split the classical arts and new media, because they are the same artists who use in the same way painting or a video game to express themselves" (*Corriere della Sera*, 4.6.2014). In this manner Paola Antonelli, Director of the Research and Design Development sector of Moma in New York, with a disenchanted vision of his work, says: "I am aware that 80 % of the public is at the MoMA to see Picasso and Matisse, and arrive at my exhibitions by chance. The point is that for people useful things are much less interesting. The objects we use every day are taken for granted, and in a sense it is also normal." She goes on to say that, "One of design's most fundamental tasks is to help people deal with change. Designers stand between revolutions and everyday life. We are used to thinking that design deals with shape objects. But this approach is very limited" (id.). According to the Senior Curator, today the work of designers is to try to imagine possible and plausible futures, and it is around this idea that the museums of tomorrow should be built, going beyond the role and the physical functions that they have performed up until now. "Museums of the future will necessarily be able to interpret their time. Once design was affirmative, now it is critical and should no longer be solving problems, but call for them. If design creates new spaces, museums have to contain them, even when they are not tangible" (id.). In this sense, the task of a museum is to offer exchange and interaction.

This opinion is close to that held by Fredric Baas, curator at Stedelijk Museum in Amsterdam: "I hope visitors will leave [the museum] thinking about the different issues raised: sustainability, cultural identity, manufacturing, traditions, craft, and the way objects function as carriers of meaning. I wish that they could see how functionality goes beyond use; how a vessel can contain both a substance and an idea. We'd like people to consider that design can be used to communicate ideas that are not only strictly related to design. Products are a particularly powerful medium because of people's intimate relationships with them".

The Dutch design platform Droog Design, which has been operating in the vanguard of conceptual design since the 1990s, represents a key moment in the development of design. Their name – which literally means "Dry Design" – suggests that their clothing ideas have the minimum accessories needed to give them form. But not just a dry design, also a kind of slow design. Handicraft was made to coincide with the need for a more rooted, more reasoned and more responsible relationship with the built space. After the functionalist dictum of "form follows function", its consequent principle has been "form follows concept", which required an equal sobriety. Form, function, material and decoration are strictly subordinated to the concept. The content, the humour, is primary; decoration .and traces of the fabrication process are acceptable at most as an incidental and unavoidable side effect of the conceptual design process. No formal frivolities in their output. When they introduced themselves in 1993 in Milan, they revolutionised the idea of what design and Dutch design was, changing forever the concept of design. "If a designer limits himself to solve problems for the industry, lost opportunities and cannot make anything" (Operae, *Lectio magistralis*, Web) asserted Gijs Bakker, co-founder of Droog and of DAE in Eindhoven. Droog seemed to find the design of real products less important than making visual statements. Function, aesthetics and other fundamentals of good design were secondary to the overriding concept. Increasingly, the boundaries between art and design became stretched.

The direction and the development proposed to the discipline create a very strong sign: a new generation of Dutch designers combines Droog's artistic concepts with modernist minimalism. When Hella Jongerius graduated from the Design Academy Eindhoven in the early 1990s, it was evident that the environmental and human price to be paid for sameness had become unacceptably high. Some of her peers responded by tackling the environmental crisis, and devoted their work to designing objects, systems and spaces that can help the rest of us to be more ecologically responsible and sustainable. Jongerius chose to address the human factor, by using her role as a product designer to develop mass-manufactured objects, which combine the practical benefits of standardization with the richness, complexity and ambiguity that we have traditionally associated with handcrafted pieces. Often she has done so by playing on our preconceptions of what is and isn't industrial design; for instance, she uses techniques and details that we not only associate with handcraftsmanship, but believe to be so taboo to Modernist purists that we would never expect to find them on industrial objects and mass produced pieces. But handicraft offers a powerful response to the restrictions of industry. It can create the pendant to the never-ending quest for more and more things and connect cultural awareness and social responsibility with practical economics.

If design is usually about creating illusions of beauty, simplicity of use and perfection then, on the contrary, Jongerius invests her skills to convince us of the imperfection of its objects. Her work is concerned with facilitating a relationship between objects and human beings and follows this purpose by working alongside craftsmen, focusing specifically on the imperfections, the so-called human element in design. She calls these designs with small irregularities "Misfits", and through them she shows how design reflects the human condition, a condition which is often fragile. "Perfection kills everything" she declares, referring to the homogenization dictated by industrial standardization.

At the end of the nineties, following a period of research at the European Ceramic Work Centre of Hertogenbosch, she experimented around the possibilities of combining porcelain with other materials into a single object. She chose to investigate glass, because the basic components are very similar to those of porcelain. Her initial idea was to study how transparency affects the shape of an object. But she could not find a point of common firing to fuse the two materials: ceramics and glass melt and harden respectively at different temperatures, so they cannot ever merge. Jongerius then thought of the possible alternatives and finally decided to connect them with a common tape, normally used to wrap fragile objects. The common adhesive tape became the constructive device of each vessel. A beautiful object that is, at the same time, strange, unusable, and unpredictable. The incongruity of the used material and the imperfect connection between the two parts generates inevitably a provocation and forces us to ask ourselves why some materials are more esteemed than others and why feature is considered a more important value than the mere decoration.

In 1999, Koninklijke Tichelaar Makkum, the oldest company in The Netherlands in the field of ceramics, has put into production the collection "B-set", seven tableware pieces of porcelain designed by Jongerius. The designer has always been interested in the uniqueness of a craft object within the process of industrial production and for the first time she had the opportunity to introduce that principle in an industrially made series. During the period of research at Hertogenbosch, Jongerius experienced that clay, if quickly brought to a very high temperature, is distorted and deformed slightly. With the company, she has, therefore, developed and refined the method and applied it for the production of B-sets. By firing the porcelain pieces in an overheated oven it was possible to obtain forms with unpredictable variables. The final result is a set with coherent incongruities in which each piece takes on a unique character, finding its individuality. An exploration to bring back uniqueness to the object in the mass-production process. "I want my designs to open people's eyes to certain qualities, such as the importance of looking at history from a fresh perspective. No designer starts out with a clean slate. We are part of a tradition and can draw on many treasures in the archives of companies and museums" (Schouwenberg 2011).

Jongerius's work is based on research, starting from archival projects and pre-existing designs. When called to design the hew fabrics for KLM, the Dutch airline company, she based her designs on those of De Stijl architect Gerrit Rietveld, found in the archive of the firm, which were presented for an interior cabin that was never realized. Similarly, for the conception of the North Delegates Lounge for the United Nations in New York, she discovered, during research in the historical archives, the original colour palette designed by Le Corbusier for the interior of the building and she adopted it as her starting point. "More values than just the new – that's really what I'm looking for," she explained. "What can be inside an object beyond just the new? Is striving for the new the main problem of consumer society? Why does a piece of art never become boring? I think it's because it's holistic. Good art triggers the imagination over and over again. That's a feature that we have lost in design" (Design Indaba, *Hella Jongerius*, Web).

The Manifesto Beyond the new. A search for ideals in design (Beyond the new: A search for ideals in design, Web) written together with Luise Schouwenberg and presented at the Design Indaba 2015 in Johannesburg, recommends a revision in the design agenda, refusing the obsession of the market towards new proposals just for the sake of the new and pointing the finger at a discipline that seems to have lost its original ideals. According to the Dutch designer, the design industry has lost touch with its social and cultural value, committed to producing "too much shit design" (Dezeen, *Hella Jongerius new holistic approach*, Web). The critique of the designer is directed at those companies that have abandoned the quality, concentrating instead on the achievement of quick profits. "If you look at the original values of industrial design, the important values were to connect cultural awareness and social responsibility with practical economics," she adds "This is how Bauhaus started. But along the way we seem to have lost the quality. It's not simply because industry doesn't want to do it, but somehow the quality seems to have been less important and the main facet has become more and more economically profitable"(id.).

In the Manifesto, Jongerius and Schouwenberg invite designers to be aware of the particular bridge-role that their profession allows between the figures of users and manufacturers. Subsequently, they hope to achieve an infusion of new ideals in the discipline: industries reach a wide audience and that is why a change of mentality should start from the designers, to reach then the whole market and all the users. However, the two authors observe how actually the designers do not always operate in this direction. "Design is not about products. Design is about relationships. Good design can draw, almost invisibly, on different levels of meaning to communicate with users. It suggests a lack of imagination when those opportunities are not exploited to the fullest." Design has a task that goes beyond art, which is to develop a good idea, adding meaning to everyday objects, to reach an extended public. "Good design entails research. Good design equals research. We owe it to the field to reflect on our own practices, again and again, and to investigate every component, again and again. Design requires a constant research of new idioms, a battle against presuppositions, a push of the limits, and the continual refinement of responses to fundamental questions" (Dezeen, *Hella Jongerius new holistic approach*, Web).

The two authors highlighted how things of everyday usage represent a very powerful means of communication: "Everyday products are used, seen, touched.

The tactile and expressive qualities of materials are important means of communication, and require a hands-on design process, an intense exploration of textures that appeal to the human scale." These are processes that require a lot of exploration and a well thought out design process method. "Without play there can be no design that inspires the user. Without foolishness and fun there can be no imagination" (id.). A design which is not limited to the use, but that proposes and reveals a potential above the objects themselves. We are talking about products that through their value and their own individual features could be narrative mediums that are very effective in stimulating a reflection on the contemporary way of conceiving the production systems and the laws of the market.

It is also through its language and the conscious use of the different production techniques that good design can express both the spirit of the time and a deep awareness of the past. It is not a new design or a kind of design up with the trends of the moment, but rather a participatory, conscious and holistic approach; and this is what Jongerius hopes will be embraced by more and more designers.

It is not uncommon for such projects to cross design with art – by its nature more experimental than commercial – and such projects often find their location in the circuit of museums and galleries around the world, as real collector items. The air is full of terms like experiment, content, research, rejection of concessions.

In early 2005, Martino Gamper began collecting broken chairs found in the streets of London, at the homes of friends, or received as gifts. His collecting continued for a period of about two years. Once he had accumulated a sufficient quantity, he began to disassemble and reassemble the single parts, giving shape to new seats, which were often strange, but whose appearance was nevertheless still attributable to that of a chair. The result of this work is a collection of 100 chairs in 100 days: a three-dimensional sketchbook, a set of possibilities and combinations, which study the creative potential of new chairs by mixing styles and structures of the found items.

"I wanted the project to stimulate a new form of design-thinking and to provoke debate about the value, functionality, and the appropriateness of style for certain types of chairs. I didn't make one hundred chairs just for myself or even in an effort to rescue a few hundred unwanted chairs from the streets. The motivation was the methodology: the process of making, of producing and absolutely not striving for the perfect one. This kind of making was very much about restrictions rather than freedom. The restrictions were key: the material, the style or the design of the found chairs and the time available — just a 100 days. Each new chair had to be unique; that's what kept me working toward the elusive one-hundredth chair" (Gamper 2012).

Gamper seems to be the right person to explore the boundaries between design, everyday objects and art: the concept of craftsmanship is enhanced in his work, also pointing out the process of creation and the spontaneous design, forced by a methodology that canalises the work according to well-defined methods and timing. He is not interested in knowing if there is a need of his chairs; the only thing to do is to instil doubt in the viewer about what design really is. With his anti-design, Gamper has contributed to the ongoing debate on the state of design, stimulating inevitably the question: what is design? His chairs look like monsters, they are deformed objects, but, despite their undisciplined appearance, they have a strong personality and character. We are talking about autonomous objects that find their way into the artistic circuit, but instead intend to be design pieces. "For me, the stories behind the chairs are as important as their style or even their function."

Similarly, the projects of duo Formafantasma find space in the museums and circuit of art galleries. In recent years, the major museums around the world added their research and experiments to their permanent collections: MoMA in New York and the Victoria and Albert Museum in London have recently obtained the "Botanica" collection, and a part of their work was acquired by the Metropolitan Museum of Art in New York, the Centre National des Arts Plastiques in Paris and the Denver Art Museum. The presentation of their projects within the exhibition spaces, represents for Formafantasma a milestone in their work process. "It is in the moment of presentation to the public that our works play their role as mediums of meaning," explained Trimarchi and Farresin, founders of the studio: "visitors (…) have the opportunity to get closer to the objects, to their forms and to the substance which has suggested scenarios to us" (Spike Art Magazine, *Studio Formafantasma,* Web). Visions, therefore, before products.

The work of Formafantasma focuses on objects as cultural carriers, which frequently steer into the realms of social critique. Their projects always result in finished objects, but these objects are typically non-commercial, serving instead as meditations on themes such as historical production methods, the development of culture, and the social significance of folk craft. The studio's work is dominated by reflections on the past: their products are not practical objects, but the story must be told and reread, it is thinking about what's going on in the world.

Formafantasma are concerned about using the design process as a means of investigating the meaning of objects, the context in which they are made and their role in our society. "We are interested in creating a practical design that combines craft and industry," they explain. "The local needs in the global context on a conceptual level to stimulate a more critical and conscious report to objects" (id.). Their work offers tools to explore socio-political issues that characterize the present: migration processes, contemporary poverty scenarios, cultural identity threatened by globalization; stories that are narrated through allegorical artefacts. The starting point for their way of thinking is always complex and layered: a phenomenon, a place and the stories that intersect in it, a scenario of a hypothetical future.

Like other designers which have been built in the Netherlands over the last few decades, they prefer to use archetypal forms, such as vases, ceramic pitchers, and tableware. But whereas other conceptual designers concentrated exclusively on the concepts and only opted for a sober design that would not detract attention from the content in any way, Formafantasma placed a lot of attention on the material. The material is the protagonist and an element of investigation: the "De Natura Fossilium" project for Gallery Libby Sellers represents an investigation on the lava stones and interprets them as material for design. The lava is worked in all its forms – cast, blown, woven, printed, milled – and turned into accessories and home furnishings. Formafantasma push the material to its highest expression, from the more familiar use of basalt stone to the most extreme experiments with the lava worked for the production of glass and its use for textile production, expressing the full potential of this natural element as a material for the design. The investigation is simultaneously a way and an opportunity to investigate the link between tradition and local culture, the relationship between the objects and the concept of cultural heritage.

Thus also in the "Botanica" collection, commissioned by Plart Foundation in Napoli, where designed objects allow one to imagine a world where plastic has not yet been discovered. Taking a step back two centuries in the study of botany, when plants were classified according to the possible uses of their secretions, Studio Formafantasma studied natural polymers: resins such as rosin, dammar and copal, natural rubber, shellac, Bois Durci, through which they propose a natural and alternative use of plastics. The vases of the "Botanica" collection are hybrids of primitive artefacts and natural shapes, which offer a new perspective on plasticity, reinterpreting centuries-old technology lost beneath the flawless surface of mass production.

It is nothing new in the idea that designers do not just develop new products, but are interested in innovating the production processes. Around 1840, Michael Tonet revolutionized the known wood processing techniques used up until then. The German-Austrian cabinet maker devised a technique to force the wood into round shapes, first by boiling glue, then through humidifying steam. In this way, it was then possible to give it the desired curvature in forms of metal and make it hard again with drying ovens. The new production enabled the creation of sinuous and elegant shapes, maintaining a clean appearance of the surfaces, otherwise very difficult to achieve with traditional systems.

A similar interest is pursued by the Viennese studio Mischer' Traxler, in whose projects the machine is a gentle constant and a natural ally. Katharina Mischer and Thomas Traxler are interested in production techniques, in processing methods and processes. They think about how they might change the machines, to what extent they are really useful, and how to adopt new production processes according to a sustainable and reasoned perspective. "We do not start with one particular idea but more with the story we want to tell and why we want the project to happen. This is then followed by a lot of research and material testing and slowly the ideas develop. We want our pieces to be as attractive and entertaining as stimulants, to make possible a reflection on a deeper level; objects with one's own capacity of storytelling" (Dondup, *Mischer' Traxler*, Web).

Influenced by nature as a closed system, where everything is connected to everything in a way, the Austrian duo has developed a textile machine. "The idea of a tree", able to translate the intensity of the sun through a mechanical device, which follows an autonomous production process, not unlike photosynthesis. The machine begins to produce at sunrise and stops when the sun sets, providing as output an artefact that can give a report of the day, through which it is possible to read the growth and the decrease of solar intensity at that place and moment. Like a tree, the object becomes a three-dimensional record of the natural evolution and of the temporary process of creation. A unique and different product each time: the size of the object depends on several different conditions that occur during the course of the day and on the amount of sunlight received, while the thickness of the layer and the variety of colour varies depending on the amount of solar energy. The completed pieces are then transformed into everyday objects, such as lamps, benches and containers, marked with the date and the place where they were produced. A concept which is inspired by a fascination for machines and nature: an object that reacts and develops according to its surroundings and constantly records the various environmental impacts of its growth process; a product of a specific time and place. The aim of the project – "the idea of a tree" – is to bring the recording quality of a tree and its subjection to the natural cycles in everyday products.

But the process is not configured as a critique of industrial production; its aim, rather, is to show the creative possibilities of alternative power sources, demonstrating "how products may be more affected by the surrounding environment and by the natural rhythms."

In this work we recognize the personal style of Mischer' Traxler, who plans production processes that combine natural and mechanical input through a new way of looking at the objects, which become an expression of the place where they were produced. "Why?" and "for what purpose?" are the questions asked before the start of a new project. This approach is often translated in general concepts, in points of view or in systems of vision, rather than in single products. The formula "What if … ?" leads to new interpretations and allows the development of production processes and approaches based on different possibilities.

The work of Mischer'Traxler stands out in particular for their methodology: the processes that the two designers adopt in the approach to the project are unconventional – a method whereby the design needs to focus more on the system rather than on the product. "We have focused our attention on production process by creating a production experience that looks on nature as a self-sufficient dimension" (Digimag, *Naturally combined design*, Web). To distinguish their work there is always an accurate observation of the natural processes, which are conveyed in design dynamics. Elements that are combined to give a different meaning to our daily lives.

The choice they offer is an alternative to fast consumption, an advancement on a future where technology and nature, man and machine, finally merge. There are experiments for which the context and the external input, such as weather conditions, human interaction or the use of an existing material, often play a key role in the production process.

Their results often play with uniqueness and some of their projects are poetic records that interact with the viewer and evoke unexpected reactions. By using their outcomes as well as a means of communication, the studio tries to show that Design can be functional and beautiful not just in objects but in the ideas they represent.

The project, "Collective Works", displays a production model that is fully active only in the interaction with people. Through any sensors, the machine reacts to the public and the process translates the flow of people in to an object. As soon as a person comes up and looks at the machine, the process starts: strips of wood veneer of twenty-four mm begin to roll around a base, slowly shaping a vase. If a second person joins to watch the process, a marker mounted on the machine adds a tone of colour to the wood. As more people observe the tool, so those people as markers leave a mark on the surface of the vessel, each with a gradient of darker tone, up to a maximum of four markers. The resulting object becomes a record of how much interest has been generated during the different stages of production, varying in colour and size, just as the level of the audience's interest. The interaction of people becomes essential to the operation of the experiment, making the collaboration between strangers an important stage for the production. The experiment represents an interesting query about the relationship between man and machine, which is not necessarily a subdued and alienating connection, but highlights the possibility of collaboration. "Collective Works" reacts directly to each observer: every recording is unique and if nobody observes the machine, the process stops.

When asked about the difference of the role between a designer and a cultural mediator they answer: "It is true that we are not really formalistic driven, but still we regard the final outcome as really important since it communicates the project. If the final outcome is not appealing, nobody is interested in the story behind it. So the formal aspect of design is still very crucial and all details can underline and enhance the concept behind it. Viewed in this light the 'form-giving' is still applied, but instead of shaping an object it gives form to concepts and scenarios. For some projects Designers really mediate culturally, which is really interesting since it proves that Design is not just about shapes, but a way to look at problems and solutions"(*Abitare Magazine* 2011).

At the same time, the evolution in the role of technology has brought to the fore in unexpected forms many local cultures. Some countries, whose material tradition is based on handicraft and whose economy is grounded on the need, are considered as the new paradigms in architecture and design. There are areas in which the self-production is the natural expression of a culture: this is, for example, the status of Brazil, land of contamination and spontaneous creativity. This local genetic code inspired the Campana Brothers's projects: objects that often are the sum of other items and, therefore, of other lives, which are inspired by the craftsmanship and by the local traditions; an expression of a spontaneous and unconscious design. Through their bond to the birthplace, the Campana brothers are advancing a new idea of modernity that consists not only of innovation but also of irreverence; technology fused with traditional craftsmanship; high-tech materials merged with humble and recycled objects, showing how the southern hemisphere can inject new energy into contemporary design. Their designs are not only objects "but shapes that beg to be seen no matter what, that force their way to be recognised in a sea of shapes" (Carmagnola, Sossella 2001).

The work of the two Brazilian designers has emerged in the second half of the Nineties: from the very beginning they distinguished themselves by an idea of design that respected the materials but at the same time was capable of unknown experimentation. The Campana brothers have ventured deeply into the material culture that created them, becoming the ideal spokesmen both of their country and of a global culture. They learned by observing the surrounding world that informed their early works; their products arise often from a process of transformation and reinvention of waste materials: steel frames, strings of coloured cotton, and rods of treated aluminium.

The strong relationship with everyday life is a steady source of inspiration for each piece they designed and it represents the fil rouge of their entire career, from mass-produced editions to unique pieces. Dadaist and surrealist techniques blend with the practice of recycling prefabricated objects, a widespread practice in Brazil, and these objects then become materials for new projects. The work of the two brothers is often noticeable for its re-use of goods, the combination of synthetic, natural and recycled materials, embracing local traditions without being ethnic and merging the spirit of integration between different cultures to communicate universally. The result is creative work that transforms and reinvents objects, enriches ordinary materials, brings creativity into design, with an appreciation of Brazilian characteristics such as colours, mixtures, creative chaos, and the triumph of simple solutions. "Regarding the role of objects, design has to have a meaning. However, objects can produce emotions and meaning regardless of their practical functionality" (Klat Magazine, *Back to the future*, Web).

The two designers anticipated that at the end of the nineties the return of craftsmanship would involve and encourage the Brazilian population to protect local traditions and techniques. Design as a sign of sustainability is their imperative; to optimise resources using local ones in the relationship with consumers. "In our work, it is the material that dictates the form and the function. The materials are the unique element that gives life to our projects: from the very first idea to the final production. They are the unconditioned protagonists."

Brazil, like many other countries, has suffered many economical, cultural and socio-political mergers, creating deep cultural tensions between different and even opposing realities. But the cultural assembly was a strong highlight: following the invitation of Oswald de Andrade (Manifesto Antropofago, 1928) to the artists to act as cannibals and to eat what comes from European culture, they have reinforced the native culture, supporting a poetic assimilation and cultural recreation. "Brazil is rich in materials and natural fibres that are not overused, which we want to melt with European elegance" (Style, *La luce del Brasile*, Web).

With eyes trained to look beyond encoded appearances, the Campana Brothers explore all possible options, recovering ordinary materials for unknown and poetic use. "We work with our hands to express a particular territorial character, to endow our objects with the diversity that derives from imperfection and the lack of homogeneousness that is a hallmark of hand-made objects, the unique and precious 'something' that stems from the manual, and to avoid the 'pasteurisation' of design which leads all artists to make the same objects for want of originality and daring. From the outset we have always represented our universe. Creating is our way of life. When we were young we had very few things, so we dreamed and created a lot" (Experimenta, *La fragancia del diseno de Brasil*, Web).

Favela is an armchair without any internal frame, it is made with many strips of natural wood, similar to those used to build the shacks of the favelas in Brazil. Pine for indoor use, teak for outdoor. In both cases, the strips are nailed one over the other by hand in a random arrangement that makes every chair different from the next. The beauty of Favela lies in the choice of natural materials combined with the apparent simplicity of construction. In reality, the armchair is the result of a week of work and great manual expertise.

"Our work stems from material exploration. The pieces start to assume shape when we begin to play with the materials; these communicate to us the extent to which they can and want to be transformed. Our products are born from this gaming experiences: the Favela chair, for example, expresses a cheerful way to make a chair, starting from wooden waste, without following rules or a Cartesian plane" (id.).

The object "tells a fictional story: in a world made of plastic and synthetic matter, a fertile ground is laid for transgenic creations. Natural fibres recover the plastic as in an immunological response: nature grows from plastic and overpowers it" (Designboom, *Transplastic*, Web). It is always a fictional and playful approach that stands behind the TransPlastic collection: chairs, seats, lamps, lighting objects and other handcrafted pieces, designed by taking advantage of the elasticity of a natural and common Brazilian fibre, the Apui. It is a vine that develops out of proportion due to the perpetuation of deforestation, which suffocates and kills the big trees of the Amazon rainforest. Its extraction that occurs naturally, without tools or processes that can damage trees, and which preserves and controls the biodiversity of Brazilian forests.

In the past, many Brazilians café terraces were furnished with wicker furniture. Over time these have been progressively replaced with plastic ones, which are more practical and durable. Taking as starting point these new objects in plastic, the Campana brothers added extensions in natural fibres to these products, thereby altering the object's original shape. The Campana brothers have chosen to play with this idea and to bring back the old tradition of wicker furniture as a playful hybrid. Wicker, which once choked the trees, now grows and develops on the plastic elements: an analogy that strengthens the original thesis of the story imagined and told by Fernando and Humberto Campana (Dezeen, *Transplastic by Campana Brothers*, Web).

Material doesn't come necessarily from far away. It can be something very close to us, goods that we usually delegate as marginal or waste in our day to day living. In early 2000, the German designer Julia Lohmann spent three months in Iceland working on a farm. When she returned to London to prepare her master thesis at the Royal College of Art, the contrast between the resilient tranquillity of the rural Icelandic world and the commercial run-up of London forced her to focus on why she felt so disturbed by modern consumption and on the possibility of offering a critical rereading of this phenomenon through her role as a designer. The answer lies in her works that she has since developed: a clear position as a designer, who explores critical issues and incongruities of contemporary society through her work, with special attention to the ambiguous relationship people have with animals. Through her projects, Lohmann forces us to pay specific attention to issues that we usually prefers to ignore and forget, challenging us instead to confront these controversial topics. Often she uses materials that are generally considered taboo or repulsive to reach her goal, including offal and animal carcasses. Her Cow Bench is literally a cow-shaped body seat, covered in leather. She has realized around twenty models of the couch: "not more than thirty" she says "otherwise they would begin to lose individuality" (NY Times, *Bovine Intervention*, Web). And each couch has a name: Carla, Else, Rosel, Raoul. She defines them as "bovine memento mori" – benches that have the shape and the size of a cow, made from a single cowhide stretched over a metal skeleton without head or legs. The skin is placed as it might have been on the animal when it was alive. There are markings and blemishes at times, striking signs of the animal. An uncomfortable and unwelcoming seat that looks like a cow in repose. To the touch it is equal to the leather sofas we buy or we have sat on, but in this case it is not possible to not think about where the skin came from. They are objects that without giving in to kitsch, hope to evoke a feeling of warmth to the beast, forcing the beholder to question the contradiction between our sentimentality towards living animals and the marketing of the dead ones. "I am not pointing a finger and saying that it is wrong to use leather for furniture," Lohmann explained. "I just want people to think about it more" (id.).

The work of Lohmann is noticeable, because she articulates complex ideas clearly through the beauty and the humour of her products. The function of the object goes beyond the question of whether it can be well or easily used, beyond getting a product that works as a powerful means of communication. Using her work to explore contemporary issues, Julia Lohmann transforms the practice of product design in to a rich and complex medium for social research. "It is gentle, subliminal, yet very effective, a sort of propaganda that teaches by example and inspiration, not inculcation," (id.) explains Paola Antonelli.

Her research lies at the centre of unusual and infrequently considered materials, which could be seen in her collection of fifty lamps "Flock" presented during her show at the Royal College. Warm and atmospheric lighting, the result of the stomach treatment of fifthy sheep.

During a trip to Sapporo, the designer Lohmann visited a company in which seaweed is processed, usually used in Japan for edible production. Back in Europe, she began to explore its potential as design material. Together with her husband, graphic designer, Gero Grundmann, she set up a temporary laboratory for the study of algae in the design gallery Nilufar, during the Salone del Mobile in Milan in 2013, to understand how different algae, from all over the world can be employed to produce objects of use. "We are using up so many natural resources. If there is algae like seaweed that grows fast and isn't being used fully, we should find useful things to do with it" (NY Times, *Confronting taboos with subtle humor*, Web).

Those cases presented and discussed in these pages, represent a range of diversified case studies. Some are characterized by a more technical approach to the material, other objects express a more direct narrative nature; others present reflections and innovations in processes and materials. But all these projects have a common search for an answer to a more sustainable and meditated practice, objects that are mediums of a different form of communication. They are works and proposals full of meaning beyond their functional use and they push the viewer to a more active and aware use, not only of the object itself, but also of the reality in which he lives, bringing him to understand levels of meaning that go beyond the mere aesthetic and functionality of appearance.

By the late Sixties, Ettore Sottsass clearly expressed his opinion by declaring that design "is a way of discussing society, politics, eroticism, food and even design. At the end, it is a way of building up a possible figurative utopia or metaphor about life" (Sottsass 2002). In this sense, design expresses itself as a medium immersed in the human condition, which follows the course of events, and for which, in crucial moments, it must take the lead to show a different evolutionary path. "We have to move beyond the design of things as they are today and start designing things as they could be, imagining alternative possibilities and ways to be different, to give tangible form to new values and priorities" (*Domus* 2011). A clear warning and an invitation toward an increasingly thoughtful and careful practice to the context and to the conditions in which it moves. A design capable of spoiling the dogmas of contemporary consumer culture appropriating of every available means; this is what the world seems to be asking today. And if at times these experiments appear distant from life and from common usage, these actually represent a first indication of a desire for change that involves people heading towards a larger, shared project of review and awareness.

Sineddoche. Previsioni di viaggio
Thesis Project

The bachelor project *Sineddoche. Previsioni di viaggio (*in english *Synecdoche. Travel Foresights)* moves from a starting point that is both conceptual and creative in nature, which consciously looks at the design process not as a problem-oriented aid, but rather as a vehicle for deepening and accessing a problem. The decision was to open to a wide query rather than focusing on a product which offered a response to a predetermined theme. As in the case studies discussed and analysed more extensively in the first part of the book, the ultimate aim is not so much to propose a commercially competitive object, but rather to think about an abstract and contemporary theme, like the stereotype and the relationship between people of different nationalities, through a series of three-dimensional objects, capable to transmit a complex history, before answering to the requirements of any functional use. The conscious choice was, therefore, to develop a device not intended as a solution, but rather to enter into a relationship with the stereotype as a process with a strong social and cultural importance in our contemporary society. The stereotype has become in this sense a design incentive and an opportunity to investigate the forms and the operation of this process.

The basic challenge was not so much in the creation of a series of objects, but in the application of a shared methodology, capable of translating an abstract concept into a three-dimensional project. Forcing the design process within strict temporal and design restrictions, I researched a different way of working and thinking that did not take the move from a merely formal and aesthetic solution, but which followed a conceptual form of thought and reflection. The limitation of working with very tight deadlines, forced me to optimize creativity and to finalize decisions. During the limited period of time of eighteen weeks, between March 18th 2013 to July 23th 2013, I conducted my data research and processed what I had collected into prototypes. The following pages report as a timeline the different stages and working hypothesis, retracing the process that led to the creation of the final project.

Week 1 – Definition of the research theme

The starting point in the definition of the research theme came during a period of several months abroad. During this period I started questioning the meaning of (not) belonging to a place and to a community and how the stereotype plays a prominent role in our knowledge and in the encounter with the Other.

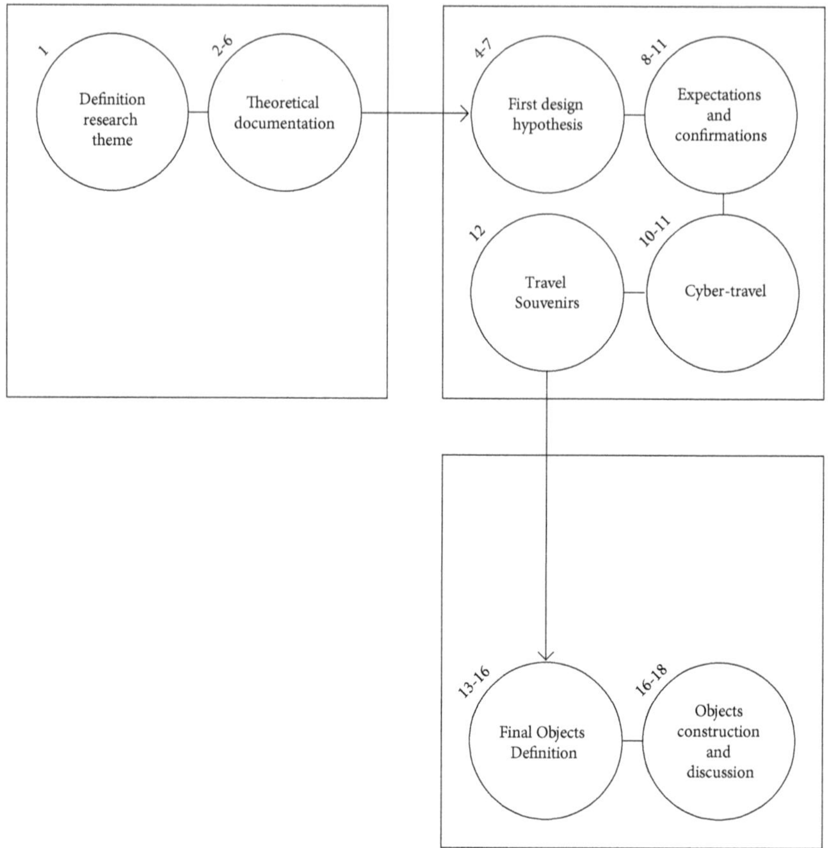

Fig.2: Weekly schedule.

In an increasingly stratified and multicultural society, identities are constantly being redefined as a result of local, national and supranational combinations, but also familiar and religious ones: a work of sets and subsets, where the meaning associated at each level is completely subjective and the different levels of identification are not always reconcilable.

During my stay abroad, I made a comparison between my personal cliques and the ones of the people I met. Stereotypes inevitably influenced our meeting, charging it with the expectations of previous meanings. I decided to approach the stereotype as an incitement to design. I used the experience as a starting point to investigate its operation and its appearance in our daily lives; a research project on the image of the Other that we shape in our heads before meeting them. A collective unconscious based on our personal expectations, but also on clichés, on received information and on news given by others; a set of processes which we unconsciously experience every day.

The scene in which I decided to operate was Europe: in spring 2013, as a result of economic and social difficulties felt by many member countries, the European Union experienced a significant identity crisis, during which it questioned its own existence. It is a condition that seems to persist, perhaps to an even worse extent, today. Since it was caught in a settlement circumstance, I decided to limit my research work to the European territory. I found it interesting to learn if stereotypes, usually static during the time, were experiencing some transformation and to observe how and if they would readjust to find a new form.

Week 2/ 6 – Theoretical documentation

What is a stereotype? Everyone has some general idea of the term and its intricacies, but since these interpretations are often highly diverse as well as difficult to compare, the term is hard to define objectively. A stereotype does seem to express a clear way of behaviour for everyone: it expresses preconceived ideas toward what or who we are about to meet. However, it leaves a few questions unanswered, such as: How do we create these beliefs? How are they transferred from one generation to another? Is the stereotype a functional part of our daily behaviour?

The attitude with which we face most of our daily activities corresponds to a systematic disregard for the richness and complexity of what surrounds us. What we do and what we encounter seems so familiar as to be obvious. To many it wouldn't be a problem, for example, to imagine a Chinese person; but in China there are more than 1.35 billion people, 56 different ethnic groups. Faced with such a multitude of people, we should not be able to get an idea of a single Chinese person, but each of us has surely projected an image in their heads on some occasion. And every day we apply similar kinds of operations. We think according to general criteria which ensure that the specificity of each case is connected to the logic of the "kind of things" that happen and we think that we know it already. Taking for granted the most common situations, correspond to interpreting and relating them to common sense, an unconscious process that enables us to produce simplicity and order according to a huge amount of social data and information[2] (Villano 2003).

Considering the fundamental importance that these images play in relational life, they are usually identified by temporal invariable characters, which settle and preserve them unchanged within a group, for an effective understanding of reality. Every culture develops appropriate measures to establish their own collective identity, through the use of common roots, the adoption of a shared symbolism and marking differences in other opposing groups. Since ancient times, the classical rhetoricians resorted to the use of "Loci communes", simple and evocative images to seduce and persuade listeners to their theory.

What we usually know of a place or of a population are the most important aspects, what is more representative and symbolic. They are almost always real elements, but simplified and summarized to such an extent as to make them undesirable and unlikely. Italians are friendly people, while the British are reserved, such instances demonstrate that a few features are required to outline a concept, a place, a population. And the stereotype works in the same way. Many common elements under a shared label.

But where do stereotypes reveal themselves most? In this preliminary phase, I dedicated time to investigate and research places where clichés, stereotypes and prejudices, found space to emerge. The visual field is a powerful territory in which the stereotype can be a vehicle of easy and understandable contents: images have always replaced the text to provide explanations with a different and easier language, creating effective memory and transmission systems. Advertising makes daily extensive use of stereotypes and simplified images, through an already known language, to bring simple and clear messages to people. In this sense, réclame and advertisements reveal themselves as a particularly sensitive space for stereotypes.

---

2 "(...) personal memory is a process of reconstruction and interpretation, in which the person selects and accordingly records or eliminates, the information on the basis of the possibility to insert these memories in a meaningful context. This process does not depend on a mnemonic capacity, rather than from the self reproductive nature of stereotypes. It is easy that facts that agree with our opinions are remembered as more significant than others, just as real, but that contradict them and that are therefore justified as an exception or a chance."

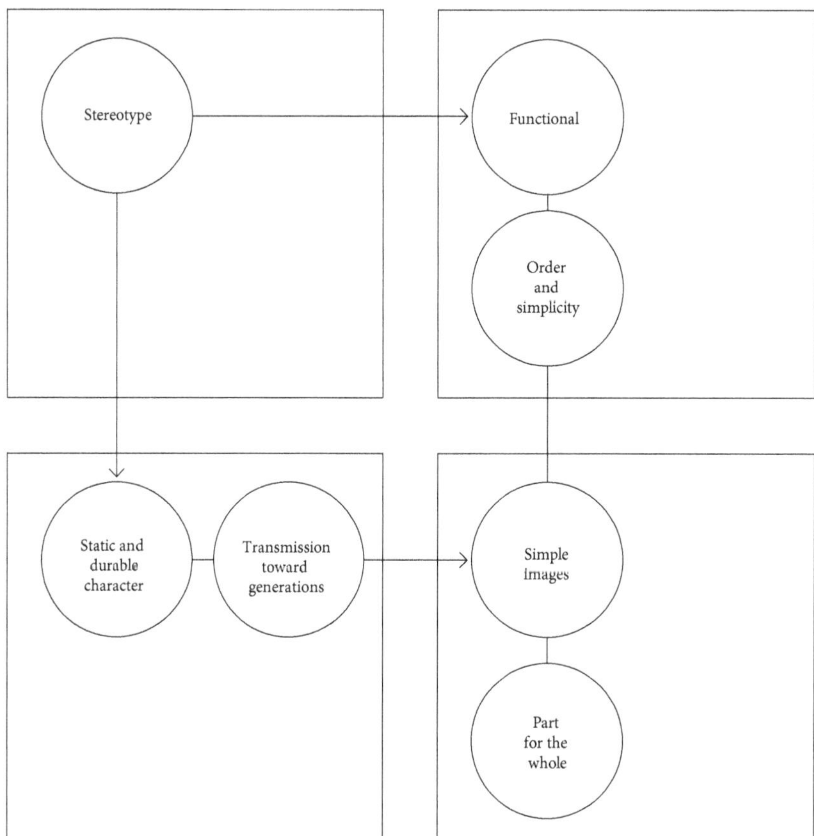

Fig.3: Stereotype.

In the preliminary phase of the research, I focused mainly on advertising as a tool for tourist promotion, identifying in the time of leisure and vacation a key moment in the encountering and engagement with the Other. The concepts of vacation and of the image are linked together inseparably: visual culture is dominant in the tourist world. The image plays a decisive role in the choice of destination and in the organization of recreation and leisure. Each person has a general idea of prototypical places, established on the comparison of perceptual data and past experiences, and on visited, known or even imagined places. The mental image of the destination becomes an important factor in the selection process, influencing the decision and the behaviour of people. In this sense the stereotype plays a crucial role: the tourist image should be neither too close nor too far from the prototype; the distance should give an aura of novelty, but the proximity should soften the sensation of strangeness facilitating understanding. There is an optimal degree of discrepancy from the scheme for which the incentive is seen as something quite new and attractive, but not so far from the expectations as to block the cognitive process. Touristic advertising does not convey a physical product but the promise of an emotion that becomes real only after the use of the offered service. It is just a promise, but it is essential in guiding the choice.

Touristic media are needed to share emblematic places with a few strokes, building images, redefining reality, according to the expectations of the tourist. Postcards and tourist posters of the last century tried to offer the traveller a summary of what he would expect to find on vacation. They were captured and reproduced, often by painting techniques, unique features of the place, and idyllic locality of escape. The use of clichés and stereotypes was a must to bring immediately to mind the location which they referred to. In the foreign imagination, Italy was a place of sun and sea; the different cities were strongly characterized according to the peculiarities of each one. It was the same ENIT, the national authority for Italian tourism, who commissioned the most important designers to produce the period in different posters, taking care of the promotion of various types of offers of touristic resources, both nationally and abroad. Liguria, the palm-treed Riviera, was exalted for the attractiveness of its beach resorts attended by smiling women in bikinis. Sestriere was presented as the best winter resort: pretty chalets along ski slopes hidden by snow, proposed to the visitor a sporting holiday immersed in magnificent nature. While in Naples, a couple awaiting the night, with one of the locals playing the mandolin, could experience a romantic moment on the slopes of Vesuvius. A few summarized elements can inspire an emotion and a clear concept for the future visitor.

The same concept still works today, where tourist advertising agencies, but not only, propose an effective and recognizable product in a collective unconscious. In this sense, in the short space of an ad or an insert, through simple and recognizable images, the notion of stereotype is a precious persuasive support for the advertising argument. The art of seduction is researched through an increasingly intense spectacle of advertising, emphasizing as much as possible the content of aesthetic gratification of the consumers' dreams, increasing the level of emotional communication. An advert with a mainly conative function persuades the consumer, because its purpose is disguised and mystified. If the rational aspect helps to justify the choice, however, it is not the final reason to choose. The advertisement message must refer primarily to the unconscious sphere, where the real motivation to travel matures. Through stereotypes, it is possible to filter the personal experience in a collective unconscious made of images of known images, which charm and relieve.

Alimentation also represents a very powerful medium of stereotypical images of different countries: food and cooking are inextricably linked to cultural heritage and to the identity of individuals and nations. Campania is known for pizza, Champagne for sparkling wine, Serrano for ham. Food can perform a valuable link with the land and with a shared history. In this way, expectations can play an important role in the touristic collective unconscious. Tourists select according to what they imagine, know, receive; for this reason the proposed image must be concise and effective.

Week 4/ 7 – First design hypothesis

Referring to the first collected materials, I have simultaneously started practical research to develop some sketches in order to transform information into possible design ideas. Since the beginning of the project it was clear that I did not want to limit myself to describe the stereotype and its social mechanisms, but I rather I wanted to try and read it and make it visible through a three-dimensional installation. The work is meant to discover and highlight some of these unconscious mechanisms, but at the same time, it should allow the viewer / user to live the process personally and to perceive the phenomenon of cliche and stereotype, perhaps recognizing personally some elements.

Simply focusing on the process I did not consider a finite result interesting and neither did I want to immediately force a conclusive solution, which might be too narrow, preventing further discussion at a later time. The error and the constant questioning of some choices, constituted a very important step during the different phases of the project, to be able, at the end of the project, to create objects that would respond to the preconceived aim.

For this reason, the development of the project has passed through several steps, which while it apparently distanced me from the initial theme and intention, it allowed me later to set out more clearly some of my points and, hence, ways to proceed.

In the initial design phase, I questioned whether it was possible to apply stereotypes onto objects in the same way we fit them to people. If in our daily routine, we normally report to the single individual characteristics and behaviour assigned to a group, maybe is it also possible to perform a similar operation on products? Starting from an everyday object, such as a table, is it possible to re-design and transform it in light of the new peculiarities that we attribute to it through its country of origin?

Eating habits are significantly different from country to country and are a formidable identifying element. Collecting short interviews with people of different nationalities from various European countries with regard to their eating rituals, and subsequently documenting them on the web, I got a picture, simplistic and stereotypical, of the alimentary daily routine of some of the people in these countries.

In Italy, for example, meals are seen as a heart-felt daily ritual and they are usually consumed with family. Sunday lunch is a fixed clique in the collective unconscious, thanks also to representations reinforced by cinema. Decorated tables full of traditional regional dishes to be eaten in company is the general Italian frame. Instead, in Britian the custom is tea, especially afternoon tea, which to some stands as a moment of well-established tradition. It corresponds to a dinner and it is a traditional time of sharing for the British people. In the Nordic countries we imagine a frugal meal eaten in the late afternoon; while the Spanish share out the tapas in joy. For each country it was possible to sketch, even in an ironic way, a meaningful food related profile.

In this way, one possible idea was to give life to a family of tables that represent the idea of eating in different countries. The collection of tables would be a three-dimensional proposition through stereotype of the eating habits of some countries. The idea was to cross and overstate some elements of the table in a different way for each country under consideration, as if some prevalent features in the use have over time dictated a prevalent type of use. As if the gesture and the use had resulted in blending with the object itself in a natural sign that becomes a manifest and visible element in the table. The design of the object and its redefined functionality should invite the user to a specific use of the table, depending on the country of origin, or to invent new gestures and rituals to use it, encouraged by the familiarity of a known and recognized object. The result should be a product, which is adapted to the expectations and needs of the user and reexamined under the light of its use.

Therefore, the Italian table became excessively long, ready to welcome all the relatives to a rich family lunch. A small table for a chat hosted the English afternoon tea, while a decentralized desk, spread across different levels, hosted friends to share the Spanish tapas.

The investigation could have continued along many other national variations, but limiting the field of observation of the stereotype specifically to the area of the cooking was likely to restrict the attention in an overly narrow context.

Week 8 /11 – Expectations and confirmations

What about travel? What is the image we have of the Other on the eve of a departure?

The journey should be a key moment in the confrontation with the Other and the question should arise spontaneously whenever we move from our place of origin to visit a different destination. But actually it is a question that often we do not ask. We are so busy with our preparations for departure that we do not reflect on who we are going to meet, despite having a clear image in our heads of the places and of the people we are going to interact with.

Travellers already have clear expectations about where and with whom they will get in touch before reaching the location. "The traveller already experiences the journey from the moment when he supposes it" (Michel 2001): he designs, documents, searches for contacts, imagines; all these actions within a global collective unconsciousness that provides a multitude of information about a future destination. We choose a destination because we have already seen it; on the tourist brochures, in photographs of friends, on the Internet, in magazines, guidebooks, television programmes. When we leave, we already know what we are looking for and we bring with us our personal vision of the place and a personal imagine of the people whom we are going to meet.

People normally tend to move in search of confirmations: the places must repropose what has been promised, and allow them to find the same image that was shown before departure. In a study by sociologist Tim Edensor (Edensor 1998) on western tourists visiting the Taj Mahal in India, showed that they attempted to reproduce in their photographs the same perspective as that presented by media travel. A phenomena which demonstrates that there exists between the average tourist and the media a shared vision that is the predominant reading key to any particular place.

It's easy in that way to fall into a similar mechanism with regard to the operation of the stereotype: we see what confirms our expectations, averting our gaze from what might instead provide a diverged image to our idea.

Numerous studies have been carried out on the theme, confronted through visual stories by contemporary photographers. "Small World", a photographic collection curated by Martin Parr on the universe of tourism, describes the phenomenon of an increasingly homogeneous global culture putting in focus its paradoxical appearance, a situation fostered by the demands of the market and by the ease of exchanges and communications. Through his pictures, Parr tries to propose the fake exaltation of different cultural identities and their simultaneous cancellation. The shots reveal an ironic absurdity of the scenarios: tourists are often caught in the act of photographing themselves or trying to reproduce the set that they have already seen in the tourist brochure. A mirror that returns a melancholy and stereotyped image of the proposal and tourists' response.

Similar reflections are proposed by the photographer Francesco Jodice, who has made up an observatory on the modification of the landscape over the years, seen as a projection of people's desires: "I've seen this place before". Spaces that are construed and re-created in the light of the expectations and needs of users, a transformation often simply set through the use made of the places, a sort of temporary appropriation, which dictates a predominant and different use than that of the original. The journey and tourist industry represent a very interesting observation and revelation space of the stereotype.

Week 10/ 11 – Cyber-travel

What can be recognized as recurring behaviours in our way of travelling?

There are a whole series of automatisms, often unconscious and unaware, which characterize our movements. They are, often generalizing, mental frames to which we refer to and that we act as a buffer in the exploration and in the understanding of the Other. For example, the research of a second-hand kind of view, taking pictures of already seen images, the ones that have convinced us to leave; or pre-thinking in terms of the operation of the image that we would like to draw, seeking constant evidence for our expectations. These are actions in which we inevitably fall back on when we face a new situation to which we can react thanks to reference models.

But how far is it possible to push the research and the planning of a trip?

Nowadays there are countless possibilities through web platforms, which offer help to tourists in the organization and planning of routes, travel and bookings. There are sites dedicated to every aspect of the holiday: consulting various offers you access to a fairly broad overview of the requested service in order to compare quickly a large amount of proposals.

To understand how far you can go in this plan, I propose to organize a trip to Phi Phi Island in Thailand, a very popular tourist resort; a place I have never visited. I started my virtual cyber-travel checking flight fares (*skyscanner.it*), comparing different companies, airports, and offers. I found a convenient offer to Bangkok with Qatar Airways; I then browsed the official website of the airline company (*qatarairways.com*) to check the possibility of further discounts and to check the timetable for possible departures. With a domestic flight to the country I would also have the opportunity to reach Phuket directly in an hour and twenty minutes. I then consulted the website of the islands Andaman (*andaman-island.com*) and viewed the ferry timetable: in an hour and a half it is possible to reach Phi Phi Don from the port of Rassada; some companies offered the service also via speed boat, but at a much less advantageous price.

I checked the weather forecast during the period: monsoon, average temperatures and amount of rainfall; furthermore, I documented on the official website of the Archipelago (*ppisland.com*) information concerning the anniversaries and traditional holidays during my period of stay. I checked some suggestions as to where to eat and stay overnight (*tripadvisor.com*), comparing comments and photographs of those who preceded me and by comparing the different offers available; I then selected and booked my pension for a week (*booking.com*) at the most advantageous price online, with a discount of over 20% on the list price. With webcam in real time (*earthcam.com*) I could already see several beaches and resorts on the island, while through Google maps (*earth.google.com*) I retraced the way from the hotel to the beaches so that I would recognize it once there.

Through this short experiment, I wanted to test and highlight how often guides, tour escorts and electronic devices, soften the encounter with the Other, preparing our imagination and smoothing a supposed diversity through established grids. In less than two hours of browsing online, sitting at desk at home, I was able to form a well-defined idea about the place that I was going to visit, and I was ready to leave with an expert's knowledge in terms of information and advice on the destination. Everything was done without me having to get in touch with other people; a form of mediation that often deprives us of the possibility to independently write the story we want to live and tell, filtering the reality through established rules and the preparation of a certain mood.

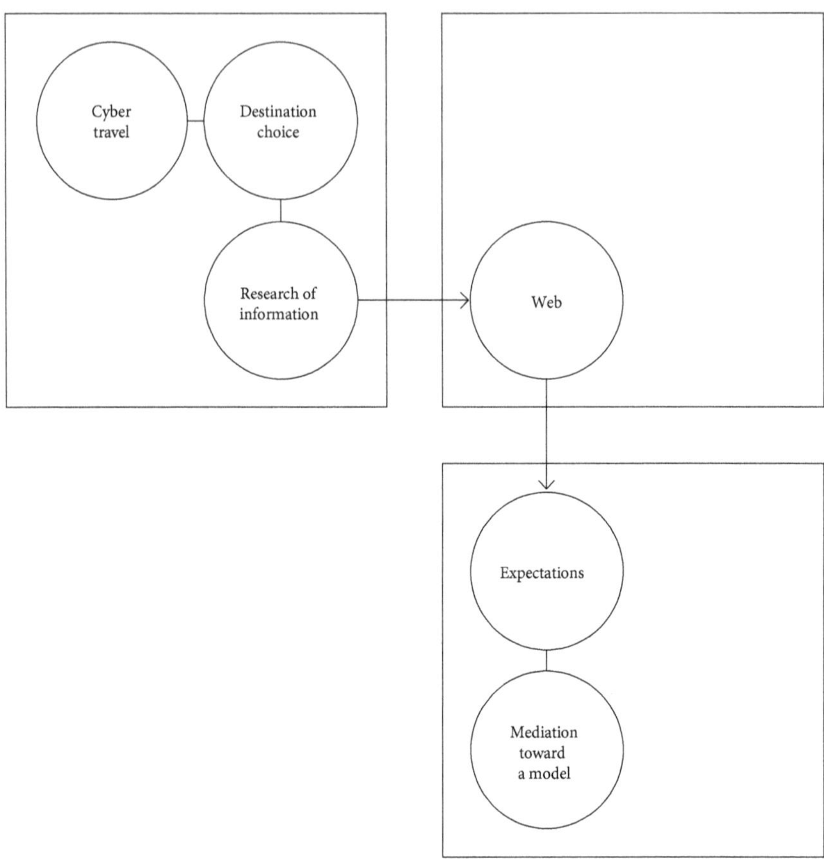

Fig.4: Cyber-travel.

Week 12 – Travel Souvenirs

"Stage authenticity" (Mac Cannel 1973) is the denomination suggested by sociologist Dean MacCannel to express the concept of staged authenticity for tourist use, a touristicization of folklore. During a journey, tourists often try to push emphasis on the most spectacular aspects of a culture, seeking traditions, customs and habits different from those of their origin. They research the location of evasion for something distant from their daily lives. The paradox which is often generated is the impossibility of an authentic local culture, denied by tourism laws.

An experience that also needs to be fixed and certified is that of acquiring souvenirs. The souvenir usually announces the end of the travel experience, expressing "in the physical space of an object what the touristic holiday is usually temporally: a short summary for stereotypes" (Canestrini 2001). The souvenir is a summary through which it is possible to reaffirm the experience just lived and where to seat affection for a place.

Keyrings, ceramics, costume jewellery, souvenirs are often false and artificial reproductions and it is precisely because of this reassuring nature of fiction that it is possible to recall one's own experience and memory. Therefore, I attempted to work on the concept of the souvenir, questioning how a product for the mass market, distributed equally all over the world, can still be perceived as emblematic of a personal experience. Is buying it in the resort enough to load a personal meaning?

I attempted to design to new objects, moving from some already existing souvenir objects, adding new meaning and a second reading layer. These were emblematic and easily recognisable objects, which were immediately connectible to the country to which they came from, products able to represent and reflect the expectations and beliefs before departure: such as a Spanish fan, a Swiss cuckoo clock, a German beer mug. I tried to rethink some of these items in a revisited role by loading them with the stereotype that is usually assigned by the country of origin and, therefore, adding another level of reading. However, it was easy to slip into a dimension of kitsch and gadgets, which I preferred to avoid. Although the fundamental aim was valid, the visual result is not conveyed as effectively as the concept, revealing the opposite – a parody and grotesque effect.

In this sense, I've tried to release from the limited size of the souvenir and to work more on the materiality and on the form of the objects to refer to its roots and to return at the same time to talk about stereotypes in a broader sense.

Week 13/ 16 – Final Objects Definition

"Synecdoche" is a figure of speech in poetry in which a term for a part of something refers to the whole of something. It is the description of an object through a partial representation by means of the extension or reduction of its meaning to that of another word, because of quantitative inferences. An operation similar to that of the stereotype: a small part labels a whole concept. On this basis, through the definition of a methodology, I established a shared process that would allow me to design three different objects based on common parameters; it should be a design evolution dictated by restrictions, rather than left to total creative freedom.

The aim was to ensure that the design process of objects would start from a different incentive to that of the basic aesthetic value; a flexible approach, determined by the original context, that would allow me to combine spontaneously random elements inside a grid of unalterable parameters.

Reviewing the information collected during the first preliminary research, I focused my work on three European countries whose political status and socio-economic contexts, would offer a different perspective on the contemporary European situation: these were Germany, Spain, and Turkey. In early 2013, Germany proved to be the leading country of the moment; a nation's economy and leading promoter of recovery measures, although sometimes very drastic and unpopular. The German government had demonstrated in less than twenty years to have passed and absorbed the trauma of reunification, and being stronger from this success, launched a program of reforms and proposals to settle and give stability to the entire continent.

Spain, on the contrary, after having declared in default, was in a very difficult socio-economic situation, similar to that of other southern European countries, like Greece, Italy, and Portugal, which were involved in a situation of effort and regression. Nations, hit by heavy austerity manoeuvres, needed extra help from other member countries.

The third selected country, Turkey, is still not a member of the European community, and in 2013 received another rejection, from the Sixties, to their bid to become a full member of the EU states. This is a country that is still far from the socially and legislatively required parameters of the EU both terms of human rights, minorities, and democracy.

During the last three weeks of work, I researched information on the three selected countries, through direct interviews, newspaper articles, and websites. I was looking for materials that would provide data about the main stereotypes about the chosen countries and their shared collective unconscious. If the people involved were initially afraid to report abused cliques, in the end they proved to be indispensable for the collection of a large body of images and prejudices.

After organizing the gathered information, I then tried to draw up a rough general profile of the individual countries, interfacing and cross-referencing obtained data with those collected through literary texts, newspaper articles, and online publications.

For each of the three countries I transcribed a sheet, highlighting useful elements to be transformed into a three dimensional image; I needed to set for each country an overall image. The perception emerged from the interviews on Germany, revealed the idea of a technological and evolved country, albeit grey, cold, and potentially hostile. It is a leader country with a stable economy, but its perceived superiority is experienced with a thin anti-German feeling. Even the stereotype related to the German people reports a very efficient, accurate, reliable and practical population, but not very friendly and empathetic. Their rigidity risks leading them to a perceived dullness. "Die Deutschen lieben die Italiener, aber sie sie nicht schätzen . Die Italiener schätzen die Deutschen , aber sie sie nicht lieben" (translation: Germans love Italians, but they don't appreciate them. Italians appreciate Germans, but do not love them).

Spain, which is considered a geographical and cultural cousin of Italy, is highly regarded for its good food, the festive atmosphere, and for its being a fun holiday destination, for its warm climate and the hospitality of the people. Spaniards in the popular imagination are joyful people, with fiery tempers, although lazy and indolent, disinclined to work, to engage, and to save.

The collective unconscious with regard to Turkey is the least clear and defined among the surveyed countries: veiled by a sense of mystery, the knowledge is connected to the invasions of the thirteenth century. It is a country remembered for its colourful and folkloric manifestations, but remains tied to its Islamic mould and to a culture and customs that are very different from western ones. Turkish people are welcoming, but the information tends to centre on the stereotypical image of short men with moustaches who are heavy smokers; there is no knowledge about women.

What results from the highlighted information is an unconscious that is limited and strongly characterized, which tends to define more clearly the countries with which it shares history and culture, as it becomes more difficult to find an affinity when the social and historical distances are greater, as in the case of the Turkey and its people.

For each of the three countries, sometimes even in an ironic way, I imagined sharing my expectations for a trip, without actually realizing it, as a sort of virtual and imagined experience. Each of the later developed objects arose from the intention to provide a three-dimensional display of the phenomenon of the stereotype through a free interpretation of the theme.

To fix some parameters in the use of formal language, I took inspiration from the prevailing architectural forms from each of the countries concerned. In this case, in order to have a sufficient iconic reference, I used Google Images as a research tool. It was a conscious choice. I wanted my approach to be as close as possible to the operation of the stereotype. Inquiring about a subject through the web, inevitably leads to the risk of finding wrong, conflicting, or superficial information if they are not compared and deepened. But nowadays, the web is the fastest tool used for finding information. I selected and saved the first hundred images that resulted from the search on "Turkish, German, Spanish architecture" and the name of the three most touristic cities: Istanbul, Berlin, and Barcelona. Many of the collected images were repetitive, especially in the case of cities. Monuments and attractions were being replicated in many similar shots and in some cases the proposed architecture were referring to monuments belonging to other countries, such as the Taj Mahal that appeared between the Islamic architecture in the search on Turkey.

From this collection of more than six hundred images, I worked to extract common elements which can refer to a shared collective unconscious: recurring materials, styles or forms, which come back similar in many shots.

Typical Turkish architecture is heavily influenced by the earlier Persian, Byzantine, and Islamic works. Huge domes seemingly weightless; harmony between interior and exterior spaces; and articulation between light and shadow, dictated by complex and intricate wood carvings of the balconies characterize the Turkish landscape. A dynamic architectural vocabulary made of vaults, domes, columns and minarets; monuments carved in complex arabesques in a balance of technical and aesthetic elegance. A very distinct postcard if compared with Europe, but one of great beauty and charm.

Spanish architecture, until the thirteenth century, is also shaped according to the Islamic forms, as highlighted by the commonly found examples in Andalusia. The following historical monuments found in photographs, exhibit often organic and modernist lines, like those of Antoni Gaudi in Barcelona, the deconstructivist works of Frank Gehry in Bilbao, or the modern City of Arts and Sciences designed by Santiago Calatrava in Valencia. It is an elaborate and imaginative architecture, which is easily assimilated to the stereotype of the frivolous and cheerful Spaniards.

The images of Germans produce the profile of a highly evolved country. Buildings with modern lines and curves, attentive to new trends, designed by leading contemporary architects, such as the American Peter Eisenman, author of the memorial for the Jews in Berlin; several museums by Zaha Hadid in Hamburg, Wolfsburg, Weil am Rhein; or the dome of the Reichstag in Berlin designed by Norman Foster. Structures, particularly in Berlin, that look at the urban project as a reunified city, involving large community spaces and interesting examples of overlapping and conversions between past and present. The use of cold materials stands out, such as concrete, metal, glass; a modern image that complements the recent historical past of the country made of bunkers, concentration camps, and war memorials.

Similarly, my intention was to assign a materiality full of meaning and value to the different objects, able to convey the identity of each country. Spain has a long ceramic tradition, influenced by years of Arab domination. I thought that the material capable of representing the country could be its red clay, originally used for the storage of food and drink and for the realization of azulejos, decorative tiles, typical of the Iberian Peninsula.

For Turkey, I took inspiration from the perforated cladding, typical of cantilevered Turkish balconies, using a dark wood, which is finely carved and polished; and copper, the red gold of the sultans, much loved in the imperial era and whose artworks are still considered a traditional art form.

For Germany, although it is a very green country, I decided to refer to the modern materials of its architecture, such as concrete and various types of treated metal, to place emphasis on the reunification and to a shared history of recent times.

For each of the three countries I decided to design starting from an existing object on which I was going to work by assigning a new meaning and function. Each of these objects was capable of transmitting a metaphorical concept on the referenced country: the strength of Germany; the Spanish festive spirit; the pace and the slowness of Turkey. For Germany, I chose a car barrier of concrete, a simple square-shaped plinth; for Spain a glass carboy, those used in cellars for storing wine; and for Turkey, the mechanism of an old grandfather clock.

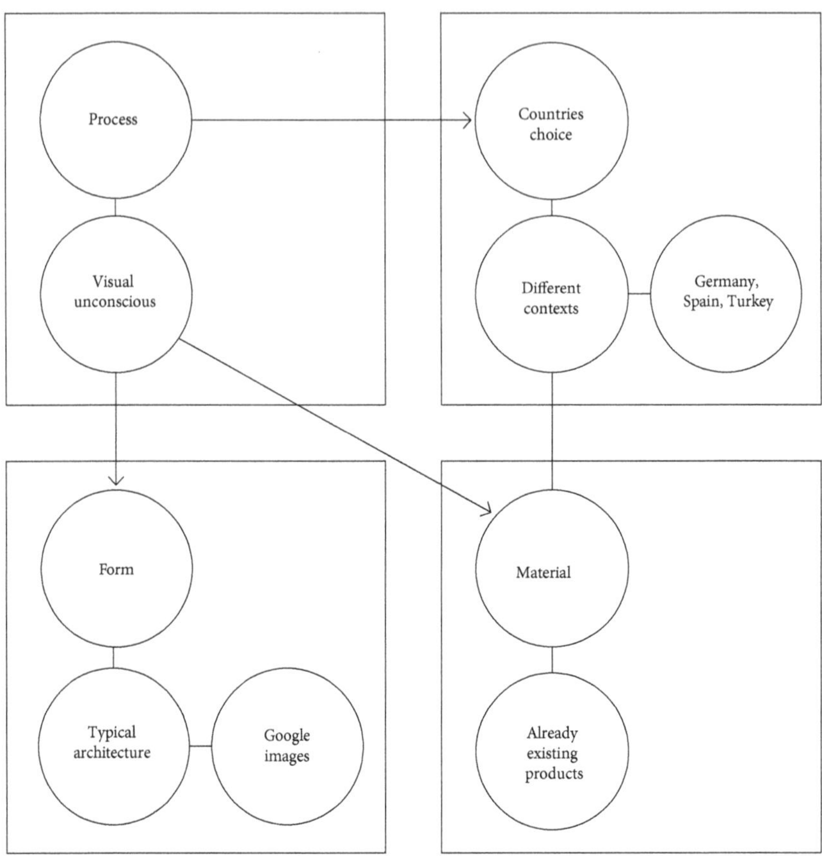

Fig.5: Final objects definition.

Week 16/ 18 – Objects construction and project discussion

For Germany, I decided to tell the story of a strong country, which is being proposed as a guide for the whole of Europe. I did it through a lamp, a bright object, austere and minimalist, with a concrete base and a long metal stem. The lamp is almost 2.20 meters high, much higher than the average height of a person. The dish lamp, flat and round, is reminiscent of a lighthouse or a torch, whose freezing led light, however, seems to accuse and control, rather than truly illuminate the space. The lamp as a whole is an object that is alienating, uncomfortable, with awkward and stolid shapes, but which also has a strong character. The fil rouge, the red electricity thread in view, emphasizes the concept of a solid and driving bond, which links all of Europe to the decisions of Germany. A dichotomy of feelings with which the country is perceived and lived: a figure of model and control. The purpose was to reproduce, through the form of a three-dimensional object, the subtle sense of discomfort and control emerging from the stereotype of Germany. The overall image shows a strong and charismatic leader nation within the European scene, in which empathy and addiction play seesaw.

Spain was represented by a great jar: a container with the bottom in clay and the neck of carboy glass, two materials that cannot melt together, as metaphor of the different souls that live in the country and of the uncertain economic conditions that keep the country linked to Europe. The result is an unstable object held unsteadily in balance: the complete filling of the vessel with a liquid is made possible only through the use of a thin insulating sheath that connects the two sides, in a balance but with an uncertain seal, such as that of the Iberian country. The soft and undulating shapes of the object constitute a precise reference to the organic and clear architecture of Gaudi, who has been reread and re-represented through the object. The clay also, because of the characteristic porosity of its material, constitutes in turn a continuous loss of resources from the container. The clear image that emerges from the overall picture is that of a country poised between potential, tradition, and failure, whose future history depends on the ability to bounce back today to imagine a common project within the European plan.

Turkey, the third country that I decided to read in the light of the stereotype, is depicted by a grandfather clock, whose scan of time has been slowed by exaggerating the length of the pendulum, which was more than doubled in its proportions. A provocation, that emphasizes the distance of social customs that keeps the Ottoman country on the outside of the European continent. At the same time, it was an attempt to stimulate a question over Turkish rhythms and traditions. The clock quadrant was obscured by a wooden grid that evokes a traditional Arab texture as those represented in the photographs of the Turkish balconies. The quadrant itself, redesigned by copper foil, does not indicate the hours, but the five prayers that articulate the day of a Muslim believer; its base recalls the shapes of the bookstand of the Koran.

Numerous elements, sometimes even discordant among themselves, that return a collective unconscious resulting from a lack of knowledge and real information have perpetuated for generations between the two parts, which reintroduce the stereotype of a backward and fundamentalist country. Deformed information that is purposely exaggerated into the clock object, to encourage a deeper understanding and the opening of a real dialogue between Turkey and Europe.

The results are three artefacts that reproduce a free interpretation on preconceived stereotypes concerning the collective unconscious about Germany, Spain and Turkey. Three objects communicating with each other through the installation: the spatial disposal was part of the project and refers, through the physical dimension in the exhibition event, the hierarchies and clichés that the project was intended to represent. The objects have been exposed in an existing space, along a flight appropriately arranged, on which had been prepared three pedestals of different height. Downstairs and on distance, it was the turkish grandfather clock, far away from other European countries. Higher up, in the middle of the scale, it was placed the Spanish jar, in a still peripheral and decentralized location. While Germany was at the top of the stairs on central pedestal, more raised and dominated in comparison to the entire exhibition.

Through these three symbolic objects, the research tries to propose a reflection on stereotypes and expectations before a travel, but also on prejudices that instinctively are nourished toward the Other, toward the unknown and the nonlived. A way to highlight, even ironically, the instinctive thought process that often leads to live in a preconceived way, or sometimes even not to live, the travel experience and to filter out the encounter with the Other through a collective unconscious made up of "images of images". The three objects are not intended as a solution to the phenomenon of the stereotype, but they want to propose a reflection on a process of strong social and cultural significance in our society. Through an artistic and design reinterpretation, the stereotype is extrapolated, reread and experienced, making it possible also to an external user to recognize the phenomenon and to be invited to a more aware behavior, since the process is displayed under a different point of view.

They are three autonomous objects, whose function and whose initial use of lamp, vase and clock has not been compromised, but they are also mediums of a meaning and a deeper level of reading, which makes them carriers of a more complex message. I was interested through my work in deepening the research and the application of working methodology, which could then be reproduced and propose again by other designers, interested in investigating design as an investigative and narrative medium.

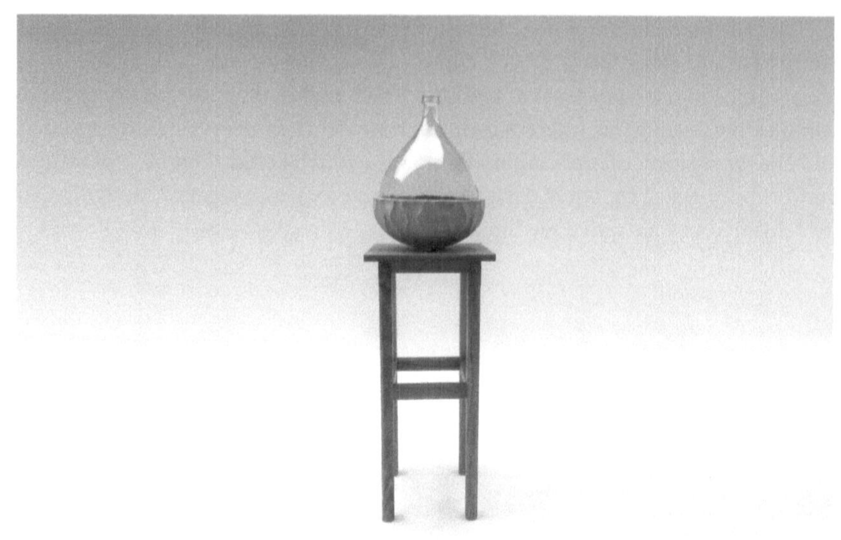

Fig.6: Spain is represented by a great jar.

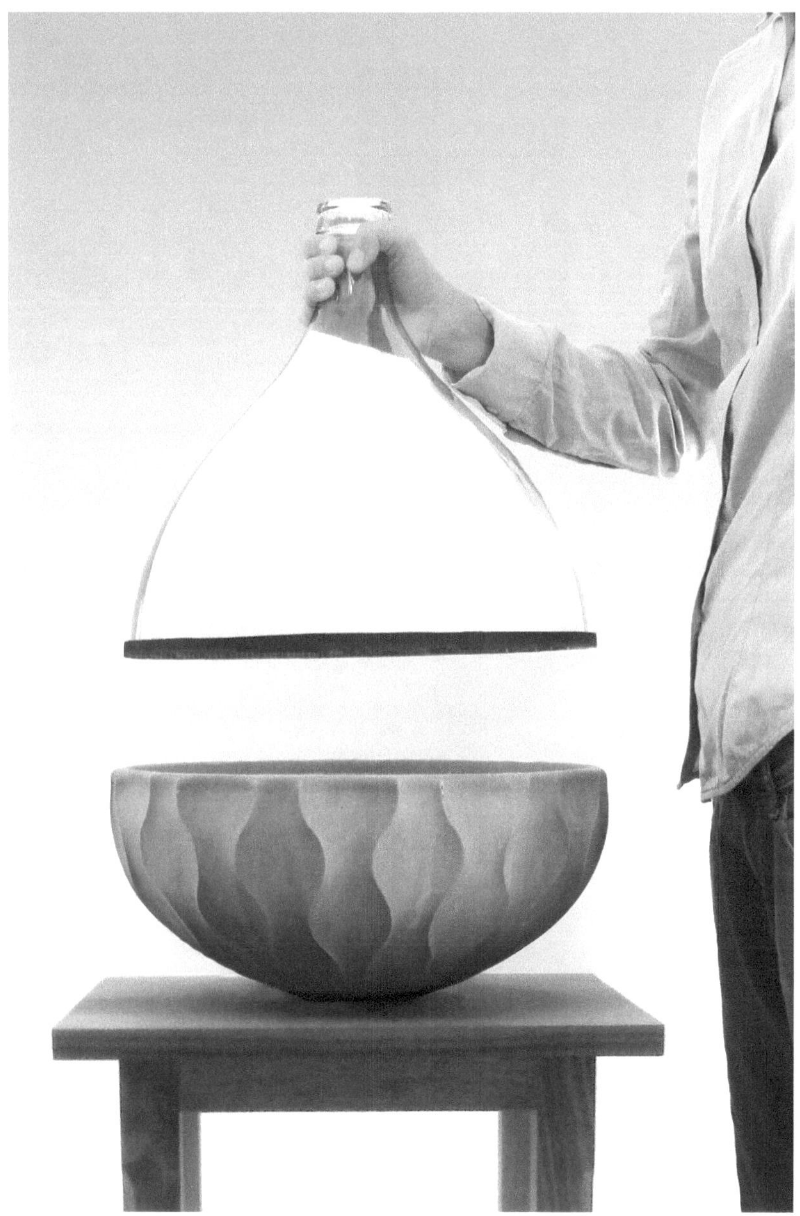

Fig.7: The bottom of the jar is in clay while the neck is of carboy glass, two materials that cannot melt together.

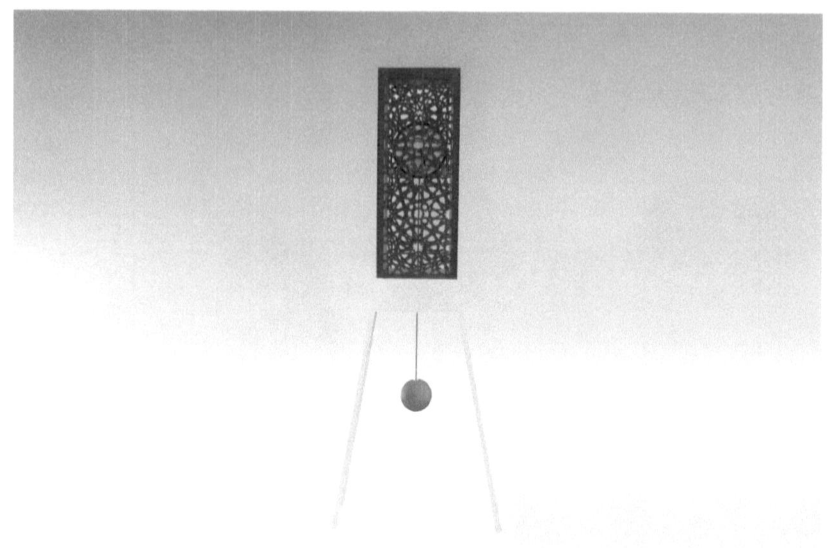

Fig.8: Turkey is represented by a grandfather clock.

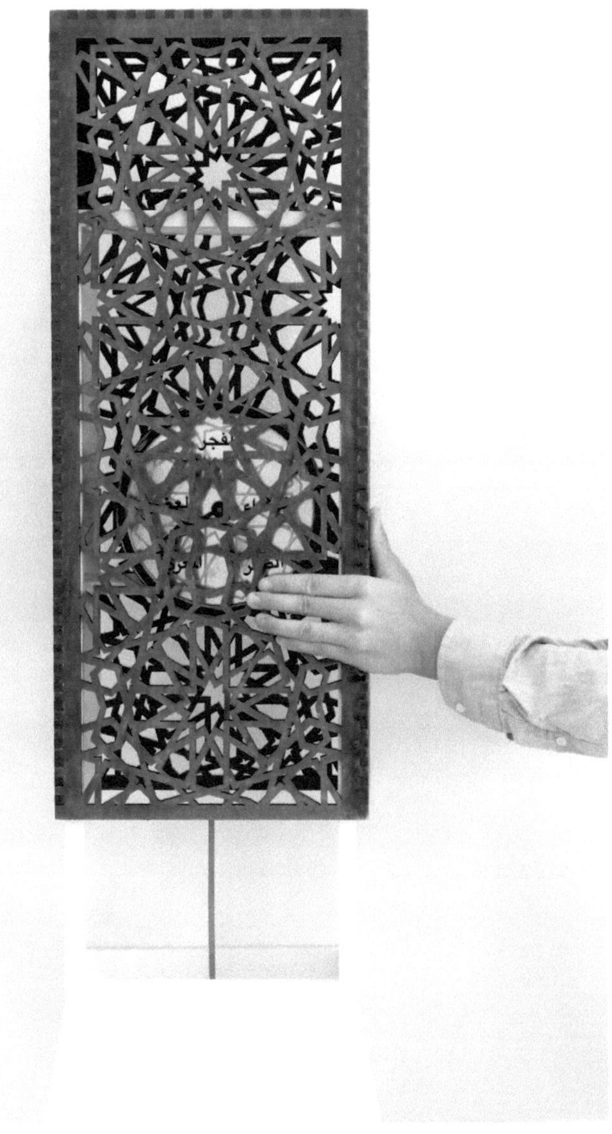

Fig.9: The clock quadrant is obscured by a wooden grid that evokes traditional Arab textures.

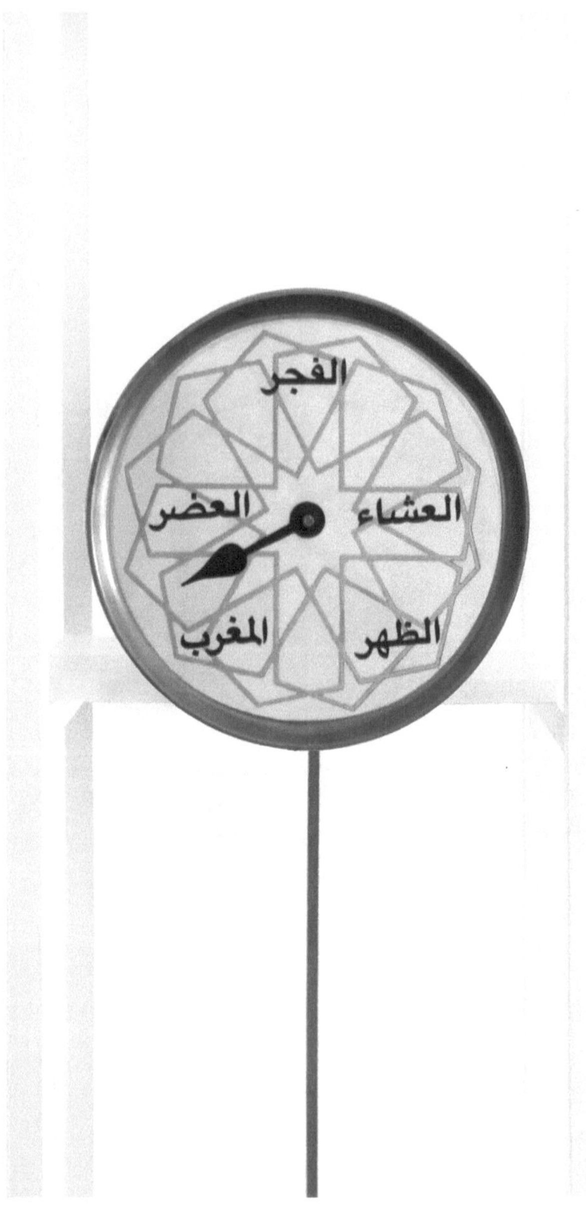

Fig.10: The quadrant does not indicate the hours, but the five prayers that articulate the day of a Muslim believer.

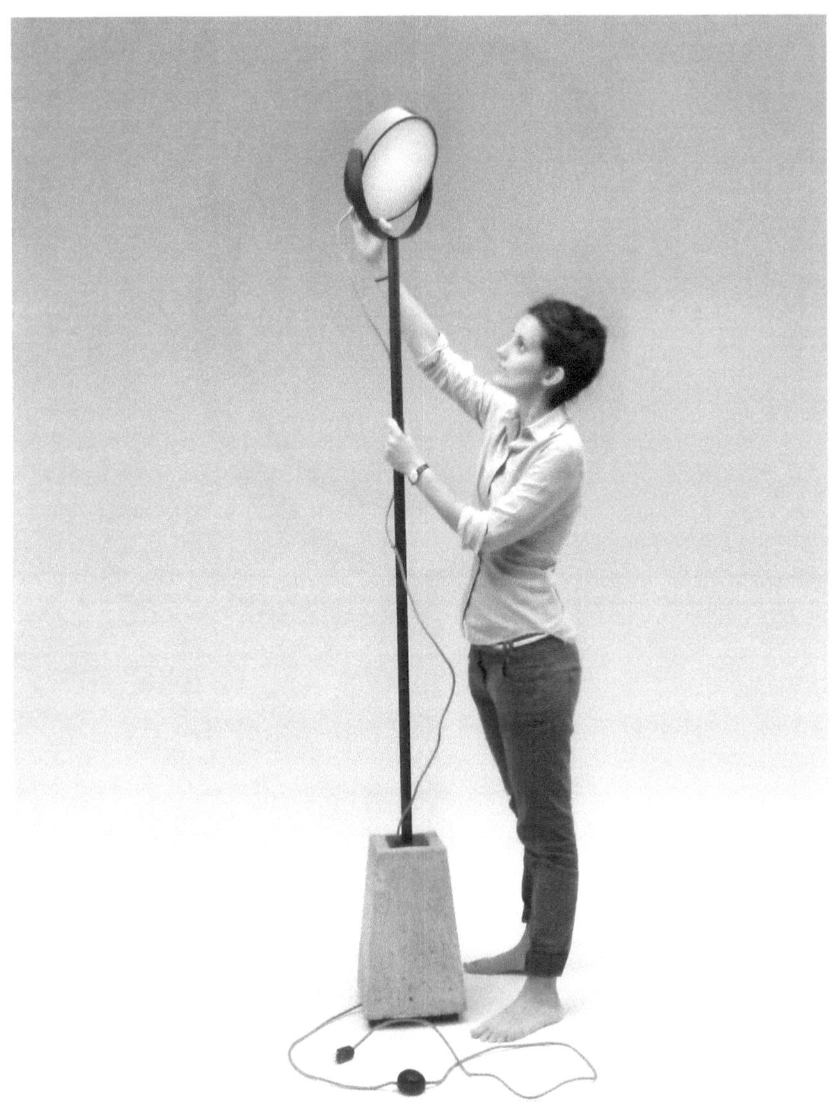

Fig.11: Germany is represented by a lamp.

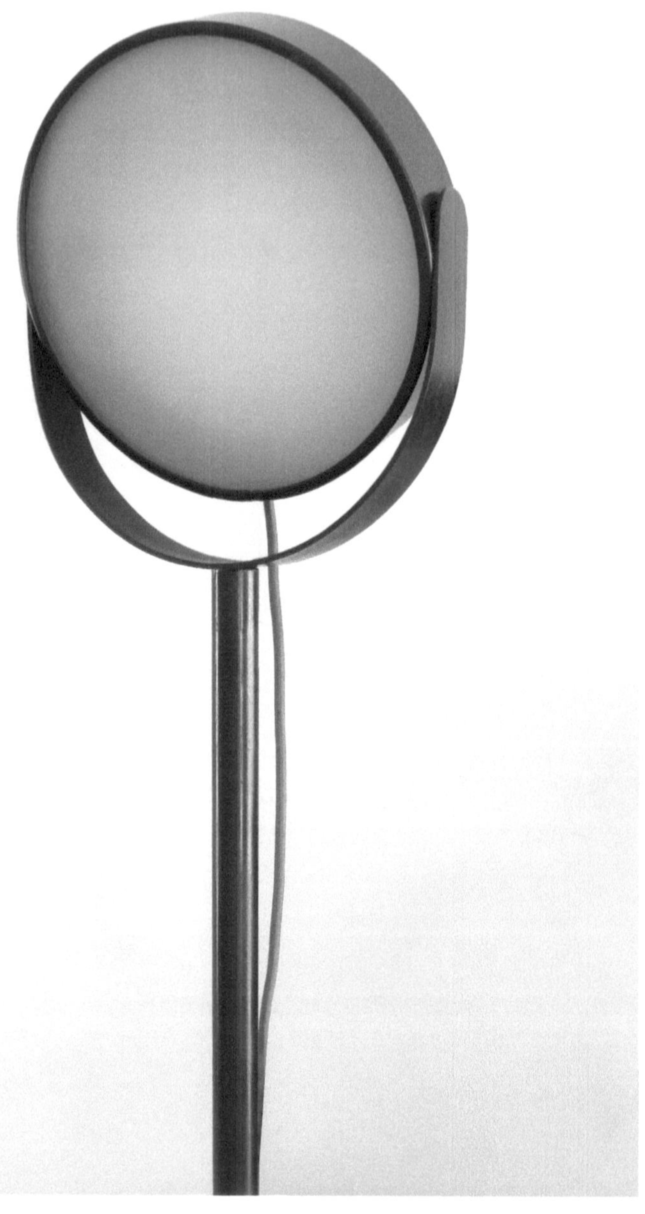

Fig.12: The freezing led light of the lamp seems to accuse and control, rather than truly illuminate the space.

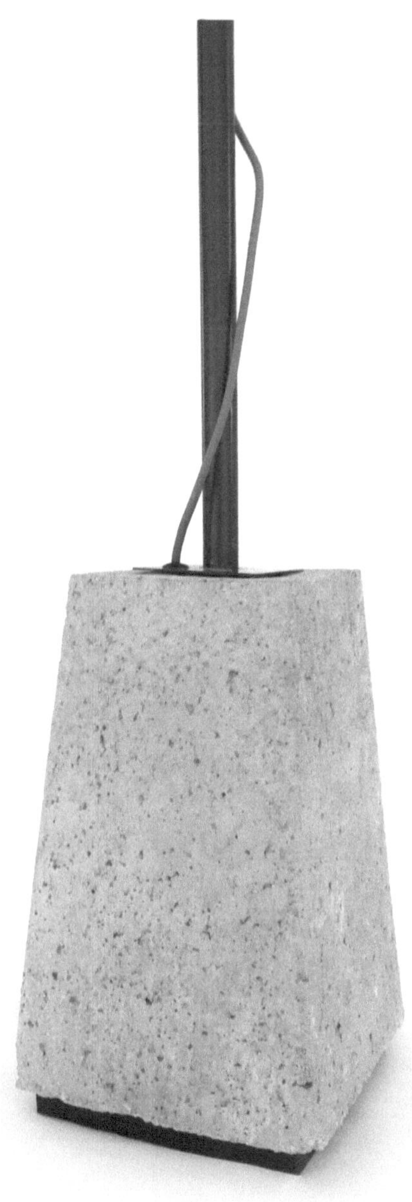

Fig.13: The lamp is almost 2.20 meters high, much higher than the average height of a person.

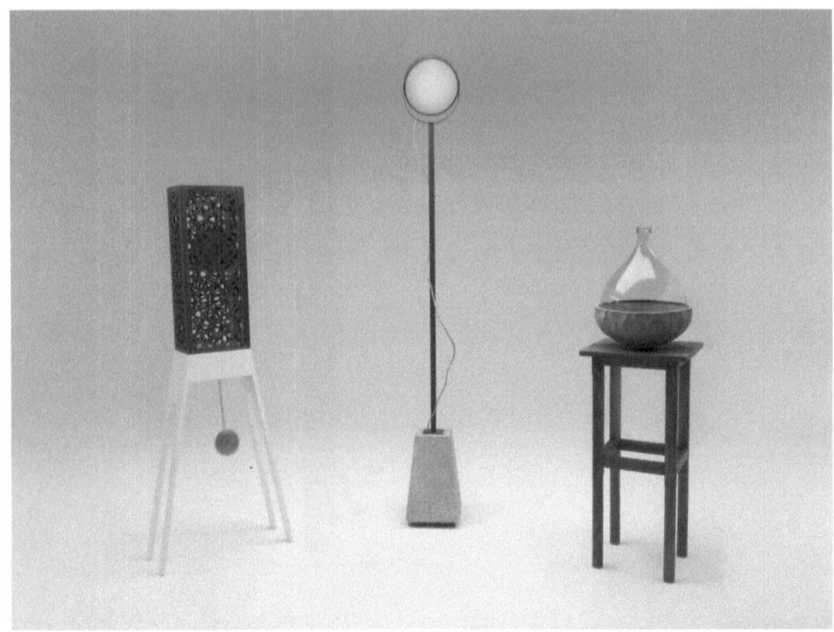

Fig.14: Three artefacts that reproduce a free interpretation on preconceived stereotypes concerning the unconscious about Germany, Spain and Turkey.

Acknowledgment

Writing this book has demanded a mindset and type of effort that I was not totally prepared for. It is only now that the work is complete that I can fully appreciate how numerous debts of gratitude I have contracted. I wish to take this opportunity to thank certain people, whose stimulating influence and support have been fundamental to the drafting of this work. At the same time, I would like to release them from any responsibility for the things that I have written and for the way I have written them.

Part of the content of the book was conceived more than two years ago, when I was used to thinking within the framework of a dissertation thesis in Design (in terms of objects). It was subsequently reviewed and adapted into the present textual form.

I am very keen to thank Prof. Roberto Gigliotti for keeping me away from the blunders and mistakes that my not always respectful enthusiasm would have otherwise made me fall into. If anything positive is to be taken from this work, that is mostly owed to him.

Special thanks are also owed to Andrea Trimarchi and Simone Farresin - the Formafantasma - to whom I turned in order to disclose and confirm the events I was reconstructing.

A debt of gratitude is owed to Jeroen Junte and Hansje van Halem for being so helpful during the research phase of this work.

I would like also to thank the Design Faculty of the Free University of Bolzano for allowing me to develop a working method and conduct my research without constraints, rather than forcing me to follow pre-fixed solutions. Even though during my years in Bolzano I have often been elusive, I take now this opportunity to thank for the liberties and opportunities that I was offered. "It is only through rules that one can set himself free".

A final word of thanks goes to my family. Their support has always been fundamental to me. And these thanks are far from being artificial or rhetorical.

References

Aime, Marco: *L'incontro mancato*. Bollati Boringhieri: Torino 2005.

Antonelli, Paola: "States of Design 04: Critical Design" in Domus nr. 949, Milano July/August 2011.

Antonelli, Paola: "Faccio parlare Pacman con Picasso" in Corriere della Sera, Milano 4.6.2014.

Beyond the new: *A search for ideals in design*, retrieved 8.2015, from http://beyondthenew.jongeriuslab.com.

Camuffo, Giorgio and Dalla Mura, Maddalena: *Graphic Design Worlds/Words*. Mondadori Electa: Milano 2011, pp.14–17.

Carmagnola, Fulvio e Sossella, Luca: *Vezzi insulsi e frammenti di storia universale*. Luca Sossella Editore: Rome 2011.

Canestrini, Duccio: *Trofei di viaggi*. Bollati Boringhieri: Torino 2001.

De Andreade, Oswald: "Manifesto Antropofago" in Revista de Antropofagia, Anno, I, nr. 1. S.Paulo 1928.

De Cecco, Emanuela: *"La pelle della città*: Bolzano attraverso le cartoline dagli anni Sessanta a oggi" in Studi culturali- anno VIII, n. 2. Il Mulino: Bologna 2011, pp. 275/290.

Designboom: *Transplastic*, retrieved 8.2015, from http://www.designboom.com/contemporary/transplastic.html.

Design Indaba: *Hella Jongerius*, retrieved 8.2015, from http://www.designindaba.com/profiles/hella-jongerius.

Design indaba: *Beyond new search ideals*, retrieved 8.2015, from http://www.designindaba.com/articles/point-view/beyond-new-search-ideals-design.

Dezeen: *Hella Jongerius new holistic approach*, retrieved 8.2015, from http://www.dezeen.com/2015/02/25/hella-jongerius-design-indaba-industry-new-holistic- approach/.

Dezeen: *Transplastic by Campana Brothers*, retrieved 8.2015, from http://www.dezeen.com/2007/05/18/transplastic-by-campana-brothers/.

Digimag: *Mischer' Traxler naturally combined design*, retrieved 8.2015, from http://www.digicult.it/digimag/issue-069/mischertraxler-naturally-combined-design/.

Dondup: *Mischer' Traxler*, retrieved 8.2015, from http://dondup.com/it/story/mischer_traxler.

Dunne, Anthony and Raby, Fiona: Speculative everything. *Design, fiction, and social dreaming*. The MIT Press: Cambridge 2013.

Edensor, Tim: *Tourist at the Taj*. Routledge: London 1998, pp. 55–56.

Ericsson, Magnus and Mazé, Ramia: Design Act. *Socially and politically engaged design today – critical roles and emerging tactics*. Sternberg Press: Berlin 2011.

Experimenta: La fragancia del diseno de Brasil, retrieved 8.2015, from http://www.experimenta.es/en/noticias/depth/hermanos-campana-la-fra-gancia-del-diseno-de-brasil-3797.

Formafantasma: *Formafantasma as a book*. Lecturis: Eindhoven 2014.

Formafantasma: "Praticamente alchimisti" in Abitare: Milano July 2011.

Gamper, Martino:*100 Chairs in 100 Days and its 100 Ways*. Dent-De-Leone: London 2012.

Keinonen, Tukka and Takala, Roope: *Product Concept Design*. Springer: Berlin 2006.

Klat Magazine: *Campana Interview. Back to the future*, retrieved 8.2015, from http://www.klatmagazine.com/design/fh-campana-interview-back-to-the-future-31/10156).

Junte, Jeroen: *Hands on Dutch design in de 21ste eeuw*. WBooks: Zwolle 2011.

Mac Cannel, Dean: *Staged authenticity – arrangements of social space in tourist settings*. American Journal of Sociology: Chicago 1973.

Mazzara, Bruno: *Stereotipo e pregiudizio*. Il Mulino: Bologna 1997.

Mellinger, Martin: *Toward a critical analysis of tourism representations*. Pergamon Press: Oxford 1994.

Michel, Frank: *Altrove, il settimo senso*. MC Editrice: Milano 2001.

Mori, Giovanni: *Le vacanze degli italiani*. Silvana Editoriali: Cinisello Balsamo 2004.

New York Times: *Lohmann. Bovine Intervention*, retrieved 8.2015, from http://www.nytimes.com/2009/10/18/style/tmagazine/18lohmann.html?_r=0.

New York Times: *Confronting taboos with subtle humor*, retrieved 8.2015, from http://www.nytimes.com/2009/02/27/arts/27iht-design2.1.20486090.html.

Olsen, Kjell: *Authenticity as a concept in tourism research*. Sage Publications: New York 2002.

Operae: *Lectio magistralis Gijs Bakker*, retrieved 8.2015, from http://operae.biz/news/lectio-magistralis-gijs-bakker/.

Scudiero, Maurizio and Ciò, Carlo: *Frutti d'Italia*. Edizioni XX Secolo: Milano 2003.

Schouwenberg, Louise: *Hella Jongerius. Misfit*. Phaidon Press: London 2011.

Spike Art Magazine: *Studio Formafantasma avantgarde post-industrial aesthetic*, retrieved 8.2015, from http://old.spikeart.at/en/a/magazin/back/Design_4.

Sottsass, Ettore: *Scritti 1946–2001*. Colibrì: Paderno Dugnano 2002.

Style: La luce del Brasile, retrieved 8.2015, from http://www.style.it/casa/design/2013/04/15/fuorisalone-2013-baccarat-e-fratelli-campana-la-luce-del-brasile.aspx.

Ted X: *Paola Antonelli treats design as art*, retrieved 8.2015, from https://www.ted.com/talks/paola_antonelli_treats_design_as_art.

Urry, John: Lo *sguardo del turista*. Seam: Rome 1995.

Villano, Paola: *Pregiudizi e stereotipi*. Carrocci: Rome 2003.

Interkultureller Dialog

Herausgegeben von Annemarie Profanter

Band 1 Annemarie Profanter (Hrsg./dir./ed.): Kulturen im Dialog - Culture in Dialogo - Cultures in Dialogue. Erstes JungakademikerInnen-Forum in Südtirol. Primo Forum per Neolaureati in Alto Adige. First Forum for Young Graduates in South Tyrol. 2010.

Band 2 Martina Rienzner: Interkulturelle Kommunikation im Asylverfahren. 2011.

Band 3 Annemarie Profanter (Hrsg./dir./ed.): Kulturen im Dialog II - Culture in Dialogo II - Cultures in Dialogue II. Zweites JungakademikerInnen-Forum in Südtirol. Secondo Forum per Neolaureati in Alto Adige. Second Forum for Young Graduates in South Tyrol. 2011.

Band 4 Peter Volgger: between & betwixt. Transurbane Lebenswelten in Bozen. 2013.

Band 5 Annemarie Profanter (Hrsg./dir./ed.): Kulturen im Dialog III - Culture in Dialogo III - Cultures in Dialogue III. Drittes JungakademikerInnen-Forum in Südtirol. Terzo Forum per Neolaureati in Alto Adige. Third Forum for Young Graduates in South Tyrol. 2014.

Band 6 Giulia Cordin: Narrative Design. The Designer as an Instigator of Changes. With an Introduction by Formafantasma. 2016.

www.peterlang.com

www.ingramcontent.com/pod-product-compliance
Ingram Content Group UK Ltd.
Pitfield, Milton Keynes, MK11 3LW, UK
UKHW042009190726
13854UKWH00005B/2224

9 783631 660928